A NEW DIRECTION

A Cognitive-Behavioral Treatment Curriculum

WORKBOOK

Intake & Orientation

Mapping a Life
of Recovery & Freedom
for Chemically Dependent
Criminal Offenders

**A Collaboration of Chemical Dependency Professionals from
the Minnesota Department of Corrections and the Hazelden Foundation**

Hazelden
Publishing

Hazelden Publishing
Center City, Minnesota 55012-0176
1-800-328-9000
hazelden.org/bookstore

ISBN: 978-1-61649-176-5

Cover design by David Spohn
Interior design by Terri Kinne
Illustrations by Patrice Barton

About Hazelden Publishing

As part of the Hazelden Betty Ford Foundation, Hazelden Publishing offers both cutting-edge educational resources and inspirational books. Our print and digital works help guide individuals in treatment and recovery, and their loved ones. Professionals who work to prevent and treat addiction also turn to Hazelden Publishing for evidence-based curricula, digital content solutions, and videos for use in schools, treatment programs, correctional programs, and electronic health records systems. We also offer training for implementation of our curricula.

Through published and digital works, Hazelden Publishing extends the reach of healing and hope to individuals, families, and communities affected by addiction and related issues.

For more information about Hazelden publications, please call **800-328-9000** or visit us online at **hazelden.org/bookstore**.

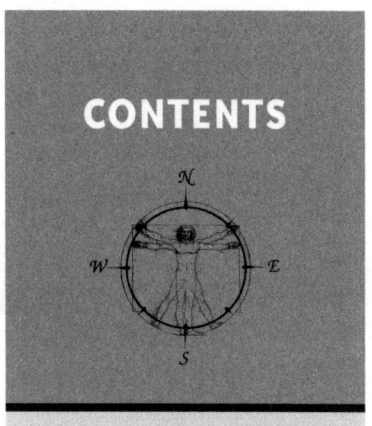

CONTENTS

A NEW DIRECTION

A Cognitive-Behavioral Treatment Curriculum

Acknowledgments

Thanks to all who have contributed to this curriculum:

Sheryl Ramstad Hvass
Commissioner, Minnesota Department of Corrections

Peter Bell
Executive Vice President, Hazelden Publishing and Educational Services

James D. Kaul, Ph.D.
Director, TRIAD Chemical Dependency Program
Minnesota Department of Corrections

Will Alexander
Sex Offender/Chemical Dependency Services Unit, Minnesota Department of Corrections

Minnesota Department of Corrections

Sex Offender Treatment Program at Lino Lakes Minnesota Correctional Facility

Robin Goldman, Director
Jim Berg, Program Supervisor
Brian Heinsohn, Corrections Program Therapist
Greg Kraft, Corrections Program Therapist
K. Kaprice Borowski Krebsbach, Corrections Program Therapist
Kevin Nelson, Corrections Program Therapist
Tim Schrupp, Corrections Program Therapist
Pamela Stanchfield, Corrections Program Therapist
Jason Terwey, Corrections Program Therapist
John Vieno, Corrections Program Therapist
Cynthia Woodward, Corrections Program Therapist

TRIAD Chemical Dependency Program at Lino Lakes Minnesota Correctional Facility

Launie Zaffke, Supervisor
Randy Tenge, Supervisor
Carmen Ihlenfeldt, Acting Supervisor
Thomas A. Berner, Corrections Program Therapist
Toni Brezina, Corrections Program Therapist
Jeanie Cooke, Corrections Program Therapist
Ronald J. DeGidio, Corrections Program Therapist
Susan DeGidio, Corrections Program Therapist
Maryann Edgerley, Corrections Program Therapist
Connie Garritsen, Corrections Program Therapist
Gerald Gibcke, Corrections Program Therapist
Anthony Hoheisel, Corrections Program Therapist
Deidra Jones, Corrections Program Therapist
Beth Matchey, Corrections Program Therapist
Jack McGee, Corrections Program Therapist
Jackie Michaelson, Corrections Program Therapist

Hal Palmer, Corrections Program Therapist
Terrance Peach, Corrections Program Therapist
Holly Petersen, Corrections Program Therapist
Linda Rose, Corrections Program Therapist
Kathy Thompson, Corrections Program Therapist
Beverly Welo, Corrections Program Therapist

Reshape Chemical Dependency Program at Saint Cloud Minnesota Correctional Facility

Robert L. Jungbauer, Director
Christine Fortson, Corrections Program Therapist
Tracanne Nelson, Corrections Program Therapist
Jeffrey D. Spies, Corrections Program Therapist

Atlantis Chemical Dependency Program at Stillwater Minnesota Correctional Facility

Bob Reed, Director
Dennis Abitz, Corrections Program Therapist
Bill Burgin, Corrections Program Therapist
Tom Shipp, Corrections Program Therapist

New Dimensions Chemical Dependency Program at Faribault Minnesota Correctional Facility

Michael Coleman, Supervisor
Michele Caron, Corrections Program Therapist

Central Office

Jim Linehan, Corrections Program Therapist

Minnesota Department of Corrections Supervising Agents

Russ Stricker, Correctional Unit Supervisor
Bobbi Chevaliar-Jones, Intensive Supervised Release Agent
William Hafner, Corrections Agent
Gregory Fletcher, 180 Degrees Halfway House

In Addition:

Writers: Corrine Casanova, Deborah Johnson, Stephen Lehman, Joseph M. Moriarity, Paul Schersten. **Designer:** Terri Kinne. **Typesetters:** Terri Kinne, Julie Szamocki. **Illustrator:** Patrice Barton. **Prepress:** Don Freeman, Kathryn Kjorlien, Rachelle Kuehl, Joan Seim, Tracy Snyder, David Spohn. **Editor:** Corrine Casanova. **Copy editors:** Monica Dwyer Abress, Kristal Leebrick, Caryn Pernu. **Proofreaders:** Catherine Broberg, Kristal Leebrick. **Marketer:** Michelle Samlaska. **Video production manager:** Alexis Scott.

Special thanks: Any Color Painting Company; Blue Moon Production Company; Eden Re-entry Services; inmates and staff of Lino Lakes, Rush City, and Stillwater Minnesota Correctional Facilities.

Special thanks to Hazelden: Nancy Alliegro, Derrick Crim, Joe Fittipaldi, Carole Kilpela, Nick Motu, Karin Nord, Patricia Owen, Rebecca Post, Teri Ryan, Ann Standing, Sue Thill, and Kris VanHoof-Haines.

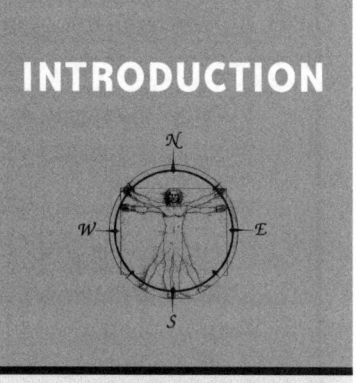
Welcome to Treatment

You may be dealing with all kinds of feelings right now. You may feel angry, beaten down, resentful, nervous, suspicious, bored, worn out, cocky, or amused. Maybe you think you've beaten the system. Or maybe you don't feel or think much of anything right now. That's fine.

Entering a Chemical Dependency Treatment Program

Whatever state of mind you bring to treatment, you need to know some very basic facts about your current situation. This program will

- give you a chance at a better life

- help you make positive changes in your life

First, this chemical dependency treatment program gives you the best shot at living a better life than the one you have now. What we mean by a "better life" is one that is less painful, less dangerous, and more healthy. We mean a life of better relationships, more freedom, and real meaning and satisfaction. If you want a life more like that and less like yours, then you're in the right place. If you enjoy life behind bars, suffering, and the hard life, then you might want to talk to a staff member about transferring back out into the general population (if you have that option).

Second, treatment is about change. Change isn't always easy. Some people consider doing treatment tougher than doing hard time. Others face the challenge with courage. A voice somewhere deep inside them says, "Maybe I can do it. Maybe I can change. Maybe the time has come." If that's true for you, then you need to know one more thing: you can change. You *are capable* of turning your life around. Many other addicted criminals worse off than you right now have done it by following this *A New Direction* program. You can, too.

It's time for you to try a new way.

If you stick it out and do the work, this treatment program will give you the tools you need to change. It will show you the way to a better life.

Some people consider doing treatment tougher than doing hard time.

Why Are You Here?

You may have heard all this treatment talk before. Chances are this isn't your first time in chemical dependency treatment. Maybe you dropped out of treatment somewhere else. Maybe you dropped out of this program before. Maybe you have managed to stick to one or two or even ten treatments all the way to the end. If you think about it, you still have never *completed* a treatment, even if you *finished* some of them. If you had *completed* treatment, if you had really done the work and followed through with what you could have learned, you wouldn't be back here, would you?

If this is your first time through a chemical dependency treatment program, the ideas and terms may be new to you. Either way, the question shouldn't be, is this your first treatment? The question should be, is this going to be your *last* treatment?

There are two ways this could be your last go at chemical dependency treatment. First, you could die. Dead people are usually not invited back into any kind of treatment (at least not as far as we know). Addiction is, after all, a progressive (meaning it keeps getting worse), fatal (meaning it will kill you sooner or later) disease. With addiction, you either get better or worse. There's no in-between, and there's no standing still.

If you choose to begin a recovery that frees you from both chemicals and the criminal life, this will be your last treatment. Believe it or not, a sober and responsible life is a lot more fun, comfortable, meaningful, and exciting than being locked up.

What Do You Want from Treatment?

➤ What you get out of treatment will depend on what you put into it. How did you get into this program? Include both what you did and what others did to get you here.

_____

_____

_____

_____

_____

➤ What are you expecting this program to do for you?

_____

_____

_____

_____

_____

Recognizing Your Problems

You are incarcerated because you committed a crime. You didn't "catch a case." You weren't "railroaded," either. You may not feel like a criminal or think of yourself as a criminal. Whether you got a raw deal or got off easy doesn't matter in this program. Either way, you are a criminal. A person who commits a crime is a criminal, even if he doesn't get caught, even if he gets off. What matters in treatment is being honest with yourself. To do this, you need to admit to yourself:

> *"I am a criminal. I have committed crimes.*
> *That's a problem."*

Another problem you need to deal with is your serious alcohol or other drug abuse. Whether you think you're an addict or not doesn't matter—at least not right now. What matters is that you have abused drugs, and *somebody* thinks you're an addict. (If you accept that you're an addict, that's good. Admitting that now puts you that much ahead in the process.) You must also admit to yourself:

> *"I am a serious drug or alcohol abuser.*
> *I get high or drunk a lot. That is a problem."*

One of the things you will learn in this program is that abusing alcohol or other drugs and committing crimes are very closely related. Your crimes drive your chemical abuse. In turn, your chemical abuse drives your crimes.

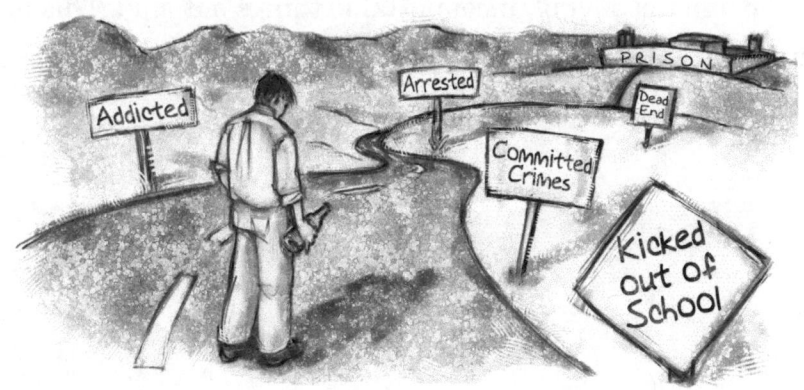

Admitting Your Problems to Yourself and to Someone Else

Considering that you are incarcerated and in a chemical dependency program, it's hard to deny that you are a criminal and a chemical abuser. At least three times within the next twenty-four hours, find someone who will listen and say out loud to him or her:

"I am a criminal. I have committed crimes. I am a serious drug or alcohol abuser. I get high or drunk a lot. These are big problems for me."

➤ Write down the names of the three people you will tell this to.

1. _____

2. _____

3. _____

At first, this may seem like a pretty lame thing to do. Do it anyway. There's a good reason for doing it. It will get you in the habit of saying uncomfortable things out loud. This is an important part of treatment.

Other Problems

Here are two of the biggest problems that have put you behind bars and into treatment:

- You let your emotions take over your thinking. You're so focused on how you feel that you don't really even know what you're thinking. Most of the time, you let your brain go on automatic pilot. This causes you to crash a lot. Your emotions run your life instead of *you* running your life. That's a big problem.

- Even when you are aware of your own thinking, you don't know how to challenge it. You assume that if you thought it, it must be true. You're probably pretty good at challenging other people's thinking but not your own. You may not realize it, but your mind is out to get you. Right now it's your biggest enemy, and you're defenseless against it.

This program, if you do the work, will teach you how to think instead of react, how to become aware of your thinking, and how to challenge it. It will teach you how to find your personal power—the power to change yourself. It will teach you how to live a better life.

Most of the time, you let your brain go on automatic pilot.

Identifying Your Problems

➤ Because you are a criminal who abuses alcohol and other drugs, you have many other problems, too. Your problems are the things that you believe keep you from a better life. List them here.

1. _____

_____

2. _____

_____

3. _____

_____

4. _____

_____

5. _____

_____

6. _____

_____

Types of Treatment Participants

Here are the three main types of people entering any treatment program during incarceration:

- the addict-criminal

- the criminal-addict

- the extreme criminal

The addict-criminal is someone whose main problem is chemical use. For this person, crime is second. He is willing to commit crimes while getting and using alcohol or other drugs. His number one focus is getting drunk or high.

The criminal-addict is someone who may abuse drugs and alcohol but who is much more interested in committing crimes. Criminal activity is the thrill he really craves. Crime is always on his mind.

The extreme criminal is the person who has no sense of right or wrong. He uses chemicals and commits crimes without worrying about the outcomes. He has few, if any, feelings. Psychologists may call extreme criminals either psychopaths or sociopaths.

EXERCISE **4** EXERCISE

What Type Are You?

➤ Which type of treatment participant do you think fits you best? (circle one)

addict-criminal   criminal-addict   extreme criminal

➤ Why do you think that?

_____

_____

Three Assumptions about Change

There are three **assumptions** that the staff of this treatment program and the authors of this workbook have made about you and your treatment.

1. We *assume* that honesty will be the foundation of your change.

2. We *assume* that people don't usually change because they see the light, but rather because they feel the heat. But everyone *can* change, including you.

3. We *assume* that progress is a process, not an event.

Honesty

Every person has the ability to be honest. Honesty is the foundation of a meaningful life. As a criminal and an addict, you may be more dishonest than honest. If so, that means you have a shaky foundation. It's no wonder that your life crashes to the ground every once in a while.

EXERCISE **5** EXERCISE

Why You Need a Good Foundation

➤ What happens over time to a house that has been built on a weak foundation? If you've ever worked construction, you'll know the answer to this. If you haven't, find someone who has and ask him. Describe what happens here.

_____

_____

_____

➤ What will happen to the house with a faulty foundation if you spend a lot of money on decorating it, painting it, putting in expensive carpets and furniture, installing fancy hardwood trims, buying the best appliances, and so on?

_____

_____

_____

➤ Honesty, both with others and with yourself, is your life's foundation. It's easy to see the problems that a house with an unstable foundation will have. So what happens to a person with an unstable foundation, someone dishonest with himself and others?

_____

_____

_____

➤ Would it change things much if that dishonest person with a shaky foundation wore expensive jewelry and fancy clothes, and drove a Lexus? If yes, in what way? If no, why not?

_____

_____

_____

Honesty, both with others and with yourself, is your life's foundation.

Treatment is a way to repair the foundation of your life. What you build now will shelter you for a long time to come. It is the chance to affect others in a good way, not in a bad way. Chemical dependency treatment is like cancer treatment. Both can heal, but they're not always 100 percent effective. And in both cases, if the treatment doesn't work, the patient is likely to die early.

The difference between chemical dependency treatment and cancer treatment is that *you* get to decide if you want it to work. You are in charge of your success and no one else's. Everyone in this program gets the same information. Use it to build a better life—a better foundation. Some will choose to use it, and some won't. Change *is* possible for you and for every person in your treatment community. Now it's up to you to choose whether you'll leave here headed for a better life or for the same old crap that got you here.

The Change Process

Change isn't easy; nobody likes to change. In rough times we may say to ourselves, "It may be hell, but it's *my* hell!" We seem willing to keep the hell we know rather than risk what we don't know.

Six Stages of Change

Here are the six main stages in the change process:

Stage 1: Pre-awareness—Before you're even thinking about changing. At this stage, you're still in denial that anything needs to change. You think everybody else has problems, not you. You may still be in this stage right now. It's not that you can't see the solution. It's that you can't even see there's a problem!

Stage 2: Contemplation—Thinking about changing. In this stage, you have an idea that something's wrong in your life, but you may not yet fully understand the problem. You are trying to figure out what's wrong and are just beginning to think about what to do about it. Chances are you don't have a very clear idea of either. If you have any thoughts of taking action, it doesn't mean now but rather "sometime."

Stage 3: Getting ready to change. When you are in this stage, you have a pretty good idea of what the problem is, and you plan to do something about it soon. You've already made two changes just to get here. You've begun focusing more on the solution than on the problem. You've also started thinking more about the future than the past. You are beginning to make a plan to change and, if you're smart about it, you are telling others about those plans, too. You are getting ready to *do* something.

Stage 4: Taking action. By taking action, you start doing something differently. You may put yourself in different surroundings, try out new behaviors, or give up some of the things you usually do throughout the day and do other things instead. You do whatever your plan tells you that you need to do in order to fix the problem.

Stage 5: Avoiding relapse. When you start doing something differently, you may feel uncomfortable at first. You'll be tempted to return to old, familiar ways of thinking and acting because it seems like less work. This is called a slip or relapse. Before going back, you first need to *think* about what's happening and what the consequences might be. Remind yourself how bad the problem was in the first place. There's no reason to return to the old ways that didn't work.

Relapse

This means giving up on recovery and going back to the life of addiction or crime. Relapse begins the moment you start *thinking* about using or committing crime again after a period of trying to stop.

Stage 6: Maintenance. This very important stage can last anywhere from six months to the rest of your life. In this stage, you consciously decide to do the things that help the change become more comfortable and permanent. By "consciously" we mean you do these things on purpose. You think about them and you *choose* to do them.

Choice

The most critical piece of the change process puzzle is choice. *Choice* is a powerful word. It is the word that most describes personal power. There are lots of ways to look at change. Change is really about choice. Change is choosing something different.

Criminals don't like "different." Addicts really don't like "different." That's why they love chemicals: they want to experience the same state of mind and body over and over. Any behavior that is *different,* criminals say, is *hard.* But new behaviors really aren't hard; they're just new. Recovery is all about *choosing* to explore new, different, and positive behaviors. It's also about *choosing* to say good-bye to the old, defeating, and negative behaviors. Recovery is about choosing to set healthy boundaries rather than falling back in with your old ways. For example, it's important to set boundaries with your old "friends," so they won't have to ask you to take part in an activity the next time.

Choice is the most important power you have. Use it while you're in treatment. Choose to do the little things that will move you toward recovery. And be assertive about it. The *choice* is yours.

Change is really about choice, and choice is the most important power you have.

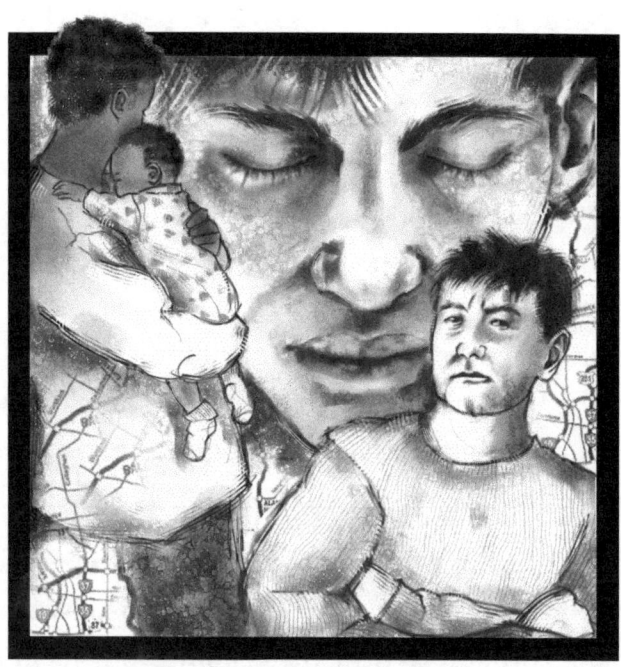

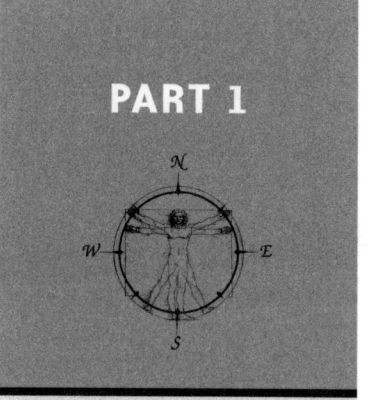

PART 1

Living in a Therapeutic Community

The treatment program you have started is called a therapeutic community. *Therapeutic* means it is about healing a disease and disorder. In this case, the disease is addiction and the disorder is antisocial (criminal) behavior. *Community* means people with common interests living together in one area. In this case, recovering from your disease and disorder are your common interests.

How a Therapeutic Community Works

A *therapeutic community* is a group of people who share a common problem. They live together in a helping environment. The members include peers, therapists, and other staff. They participate in each other's growth and healing. This is done so that each group member has a full opportunity to solve that common problem for himself. Every member of the community is there to help each other. You'll be helping each other recover from your addiction to criminal behavior and alcohol and other drugs. You'll also look at some of the thinking that led you into and keeps you in those addictions. What you are all after is a better life.

In this program, you *are* your brother's keeper. That is, you are all responsible to each other. There is no such thing as cruising through treatment, keeping your head down, and doing your time. In treatment, you are expected to make an effort and to open up to others. You are part of a community where you will be expected to do things that

- make the community stronger, not weaker

- model healthy behavior for others

- move yourself and your group members toward sober, responsible living

- keep your eyes on the prize of a better life both for yourself and for your treatment brothers

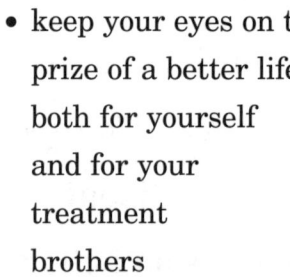

Your Therapeutic Community

➤ Write down the name of your new community here. Then, fill in the names of all the communities of which you are now a part.

Program name: _____

_____

Institution name: _____

_____

State: _____

Country: _____

Planet: _____

This is your new home. Starting today, you are responsible for doing whatever you can every day to make every level of your community—from your unit to the whole planet—healthy and whole. You will need to start with yourself. Until you start getting healthy, you're no good to anyone or anything else.

Creating Real Community

You and your peers each come from different communities and have different life experiences. It doesn't matter what the color of your skin is, whether you are rich or poor, or where you come from. The point is you have a lot more in common with each other than you think. You are all criminals and addicts.

**You are much more alike
than you are different.**

In treatment, you leave your other communities behind. These other communities include the general population of this correctional facility and any gang affiliation. They also include your friends and associates inside and outside the walls. While you are in treatment, your treatment brothers—called "peers," which means equals—are your gang, your family, and your friends. For now, your loyalty is to them. That means you will have to do two things:

1. Leave any gang affiliation at the door.

2. Replace the criminal code with a responsibility code.

Taking these two steps may be difficult, but you must do them to succeed in treatment.

Leaving Your Gang Affiliation at the Door

If you have been a member of a gang while either incarcerated or on the street, no one is asking you to quit the gang or betray it. What you're being asked to do is put your membership on hold for the time you are here. Check it at the door like you might check a coat. If you want to pick it up again when you leave this program, that will be up to you. You cannot be in a therapeutic community and be active in a gang at the same time.

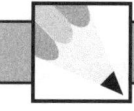

Your Treatment Agreement

➤ Complete and sign the following contract. This contract is an agreement between you, your peers, and the staff of this program. It carries no legal authority. Only you can enforce it, though your peers might call you on it if they think you're acting in a way that violates this agreement—and they should. Even if you are not in a gang, fill out and sign this agreement anyway. It's still a statement of your commitment to your peers in the therapeutic community.

My Treatment Agreement

I, _____
(NAME)

    agree to leave all gang or other group affiliations and loyalties at the door for the time I am in treatment, approximately the next _____ weeks / months (circle one).

I understand that I may pick up those affiliations or not when I leave treatment. It will be my choice. For now, however, my affiliation is with the men in

_____
(UNIT NAME OR NUMBER)

_____
(NAME OF TREATMENT PROGRAM)

Signed,

_____
(YOUR SIGNATURE AND TODAY'S DATE)

Breaking the Criminal Code

Among criminals, there is an unwritten code. One big part of that code goes something like this: "Never snitch on someone else. Keep your information close and your mouth shut. Never help 'the Man.'"

EXERCISE **8** EXERCISE

Defining the Criminal Code

➤ You may have other rules in mind that are part of the criminal code. Talk about this with your peers, and then write more of the unwritten rules of being a criminal in the space below. One example might be:

"I lie because it's easy. Honest people are chumps, and I'm no chump."

1. _____

2. _____

3. _____

4. _____

5. _____

6. _____

7. _____

8. _____

9. _____

10. _____

To be successful in this program, you need to follow a "responsibility code." It states the following:

1. Confronting criminal and addictive thinking and behavior out loud in group isn't snitching. It's refusing to let your brother get away with the kind of BS that will take him right back to chemicals and crime.

2. Telling the truth about yourself and your history to peers and staff isn't a sign of weakness; it's a sign of strength and courage.

3. Trying to be open and honest doesn't make you a punk. Lying or withholding information to protect yourself or someone else does make you a punk. That kind of protection only guarantees that no one will ever get better—not them and not you.

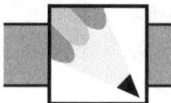 **EXERCISE 9 EXERCISE**

Creating a Responsibility Code

➤ With another peer or in a small group, come up with more suggestions for the responsibility code. Write those suggestions here. Then discuss them with your group.

1. _____

2. _____

3. _____

4. _____

5. _____

How a Group Works

Much of the work you will do in treatment will happen in small or large groups with your peers. You have a responsibility to follow certain rules in your group.

Rules of Behavior in Group

The following rules must be followed in order for group sessions to work in a therapeutic way:

1. **Be on time for group, and be prepared to stay in group.**

   - Take care of restroom needs before group starts.

   - Never leave group except for a very good reason and only with staff approval.

2. **No side conversations or distracting activity.**

   - Focus on the speaker.

   - Don't whisper or talk to only one person. If you have something to say, say it to the group.

   - Don't slouch, lean back in your chair, close your eyes, or watch something going on outside the group.

   - No playing with notebooks, pens, papers, or anything else.

3. **No gossiping about another person; no talking about others unless they are present.**

   - If you need to pull someone up (challenge them or call them on some unhealthy behavior), have the courage and respect to do it in group in front of that peer.

4. **All feelings may be expressed.**

   - Everybody's feelings are worthwhile and worth dealing with if they are sincere.

Your Responsibilities in Group

Some of your responsibilities as a member of the group are to do the following:

1. **Listen first, speak second.**

   - You were given two eyes, two ears, and only one mouth for a reason: watch and listen at least four times as much as you speak.

   - Pay attention when others are talking. Keep an attentive posture.

   - Don't cut people short to defend yourself—listen until they are finished.

   - When you do speak, work on maintaining eye contact with the person or people you're talking to.

2. **Come to group prepared and ready to participate.**

   - Do all your assignments *before* group.

   - Always show up to group on time.

   - Do not stay silent. Give feedback even if you don't think you have anything new to add. You can always agree with something someone else said or just offer your support, or you can identify from your own experience.

3. **Encourage others to participate.**

   - It's the group's responsibility to make sure everyone is involved. Be a leader by encouraging others to speak and making sure everyone has a chance to do so.

   - Be respectful of the values, beliefs, and opinions of others.

Be respectful of the values, beliefs, and opinions of others.

4. **Ask for group time if you need help with something in particular.**

- Always ask for group time at the beginning of group, not at the end.

- Be specific, clear, and to the point in stating your issues. Don't get bogged down in unnecessary details.

- Tell the group up front what you hope to gain from your group time.

- Be honest and straightforward. Don't waste everybody's time.

- Be prepared to listen to feedback without getting defensive.

- Keep the focus on *your* feelings, *your* thoughts, *your* self-talk, and *your* behavior. Your using patterns, criminal activity, self-defeating behaviors, negative attitudes, distorted thoughts, drug cravings, or anger issues are all appropriate areas of discussion. Group time is not a gripe session about someone else.

Giving and Receiving Feedback

We've already discussed how in a therapeutic community, you are responsible for your peers and each of them is responsible for you. To carry out this responsibility, you must learn how to give and receive **feedback.**

When you give feedback, you may be telling one of your peers that he is not following the community rules or practicing the thinking and behavior changes required for a sober, crime-free life. In such a case, you are telling him that he is hurting the community and himself. Feedback is the way you call this issue to his attention and ask him to make some changes.

Feedback

When one peer challenges or supports another peer's behavior or language, it's called *feedback.*

Feedback can also be used to tell a peer he is doing well, working hard, and showing healthy changes.

Feedback is about caring and respect. It can be done inside or outside of group.

But while peers in a therapeutic community must look out for each other, they must also learn how to challenge each other. To do this, you need to learn right away what feedback *is* and what it *is not*.

What Feedback IS:

- Feedback *is* directed at another's behavior.

- Feedback *is* trying to help guide another person back on the path to sober, crime-free living by holding him accountable.

- Feedback *is* offering information from a different perspective so that another person might see reality more clearly.

- Feedback *is* an effort to make your community stronger by making it healthier.

- Feedback *is* an opportunity to own up to your own faults when you challenge the faults of another.

- Feedback *is* done out of sincere concern for another's well-being. You do it because you care.

- Feedback *is* a way to show true respect for another.

- Feedback *is* what you expect other peers to do for you when your thinking, speaking, or behavior slips back into addictive and criminal modes.

When we say that peers are responsible for each other, however, we don't mean they should try to control or manipulate each other's actions. *You can't change anyone except yourself.* That is true for everyone in the community. That's why you *are not responsible* for forcing other peers to act in a certain way. Feedback *is not* about controlling others.

What Feedback IS NOT:

- Feedback *is not* directed at another person's character. (Feedback looks at what you do, not who you are.)

- Feedback *is not* trying to shame another person. (Everybody is going to make mistakes.)

- Feedback *is not* trying to control another person, to force your will on him. (You'll be busy enough trying to control *yourself*.)

- Feedback *is not* a way to feed your ego, to show that you're somehow better than someone else. (You're not.)

- Feedback *is not* one person attacking or trying to humiliate another. (Beware: what goes around tends to come around.)

- Feedback *is not* a way to keep the focus off of yourself by trying to put it on someone else. (That's a common criminal tactic, so it won't help you or anyone else move toward recovery.)

Guidelines for Giving Good Feedback

1. **Describe, don't label.** Describe your own reaction, don't make a judgment that puts the speaker on the defensive. Speak from your own experience. Avoid abusive language of any kind.

2. **Be specific rather than general.** Instead of saying, "You're always going around being aggressive," give the details of what happened, how you felt, and what you thought about it. Say, "Last night when I confronted you about being too noisy, you just glared at me and stomped off. It seemed pretty aggressive and felt like you were blowing me off."

3. **Direct your feedback toward thinking and behavior that the receiver can do something about.** It's pretty frustrating to

be reminded of a fault over which one has no control. Focus on what the peer *can* change, and offer suggestions on *how* he might change.

4. **Keep feedback as fresh as possible.**
Feedback loses its value as time passes between an incident and the discussion in group. Bring things up in a timely manner, but in a setting that provides support and resolution. This might be in a group or a community meeting.

5. **Check out your feedback by asking others what they are hearing.** If you're not sure you're communicating clearly, you can ask the receiver to repeat what you just said in his own words. You can also ask the group to do this and comment on whether your words were clear.

6. **Confront others from a base of trust.**
Confrontation is when someone brings up contradictions in what another person has said. These discrepancies may be between

- what he thinks and what he says

- how he feels and what he says

- what he says and what he does

- his words and his body language

- his self-image and how he is seen by others

- the life he lives and the life he would like to live

Confrontation is not an attack. There needs to be some trust and understanding between the person confronting and the person confronted. Only one thing should be pointed out at one time. This prevents the confronted person from being overwhelmed. It's a good idea to reassure the person being confronted that you are only doing it to help him.

Feedback is about caring and respect. It can be done inside or outside of a group.

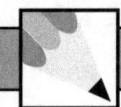

Receiving Feedback

➤ Now that you know what feedback is about, how will you handle feedback when one of your peers pulls *you* up (challenges you on your behavior) and holds *you* accountable for something? In the sections below, list *appropriate* and *inappropriate* ways of taking feedback from others.

What are appropriate ways of receiving feedback?

1. _____

2. _____

3. _____

4. _____

5. _____

What are inappropriate ways of receiving feedback?

1. _____

2. _____

3. _____

4. _____

5. _____

Feedback is an opportunity to own up to your own faults when you challenge the faults of another.

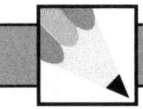

Making Group Feedback Sessions Work

➤ As a group, brainstorm ideas of what makes a therapeutic community group session work well. List the ideas that you and your group come up with here:

1. _____

2. _____

3. _____

4. _____

5. _____

6. _____

7. _____

8. _____

9. _____

10. _____

➤ Why are these things important? What might happen in group if these things weren't there? If necessary, complete this exercise in a notebook or in the notes section of this workbook.

_____

_____

Disclosing

Disclosing means sharing truthfully and openly in group. You can't come to know yourself if you don't open up with your peers and get their feedback. You can't change in healthy ways if you don't come to know yourself better. Disclosing is at the center of the treatment process.

Telling your story and the truth about yourself in front of others won't be easy or comfortable at first. Everyone carries around stuff they'd rather not bring up. You'll see how others do it and then go from there. You *don't* have to tell everyone absolutely everything about yourself. But you *do* have to be honest and open about what holds you back from leaving the addictive and criminal life behind.

Disclosing

Disclosing is the act of telling others about yourself. When you are honest about where you've been, what you've done, and what you like and dislike about yourself, this is disclosing.

One-on-One: Practice Disclosing

➤ To be a part of a new treatment community, you will have to get used to telling others about yourself. You will also need to listen closely while others tell you about themselves.

It is very important that you learn to disclose to your peers. During the orientation period, your staff leader will ask you to meet with another person or group of people for at least ten minutes. Tell your story: who you are, where you came from, what you've done, how you feel, what you think, and what you would like to have happen in your life. If they volunteer to share their stories with you, listen to them carefully.

Get to know these people. You don't have to become friends —you don't even have to like them. You do have to accept them as part of your community. Ask five of these peers to sign their names and the date below to show that they have heard your story.

	Name	Date
1.	_____	_____
2.	_____	_____
3.	_____	_____
4.	_____	_____
5.	_____	_____

Rules, Responsibilities, and Expectations

There are very clear rules, responsibilities, and expectations in this therapeutic community treatment program. They may be quite different from those in the general population. How well you understand and live by them will have a lot to do with your chances of getting healthier. Breaking rules uses up time and energy and shows the community that you are not moving toward recovery. When that happens, you are wasting your time, the staff's time, and the time of your peers. Fighting everything and everyone or playing games by trying to get one over on security or treatment staff is not worth it. If this is what you are planning, do yourself and everyone else a favor and transfer out (if that is an option for you).

The rules and regulations of your living unit, this specific treatment program, and the correctional facility in which you are incarcerated are unique. The staff will give you a list of rules for your correctional facility. There are rules, responsibilities, and expectations that all therapeutic communities have in common.

Rules of a Therapeutic Community

1. Absolutely no use, transportation, or possession of drugs or alcohol on or off the unit. This includes *all* contraband.

2. Absolutely no assaults or dangerous acts of physical violence and no threats of assaults or dangerous acts of physical violence, including veiled (or "sideways") threats.

3. Absolutely no verbal abuse in any form.

4. Absolutely no sexual behavior with others or sexual acting out in any manner.

5. You must be on time for all group meetings, individual sessions, appointments, and activities.

6. Absolutely no statements or messages with prejudicial (bigoted) overtones regarding any group's or individual's racial or ethnic background or sexual orientation.

7. No use of street names or nicknames in treatment. Address one another as "Mr. [last name]" or, in the case of female staff, "Ms. [last name]."

8. Comply with all policies, rules, and expectations of the correctional facility and your unit.

9. Absolutely no tampering with any security device: locks, chains, fencing, windows, screens, doors, walls, and so on.

10. Urine analyses (UAs) will take place throughout the treatment process.

Responsibilities in the Therapeutic Community

1. Follow the directions and advice offered by staff.

2. Know the staff who are caring for you.

3. Report changes in your condition to those responsible for your care and welfare.

4. Use the grievance procedure if you feel your rights are being violated.

5. Keep all appointments, and cooperate with staff.

6. Relate incidents that could be harmful to your and/or your peers' treatment program.

7. Take an active part in all group, community, and therapy sessions.

Expectations of the Therapeutic Community

There are some major expectations for your behavior in the therapeutic community. It's important to read the following expectations carefully, discuss them with your peers, and ask therapists questions about them. You need to understand what they're all about. Be prepared to live up to these expectations.

1. **Keep it real.**

   - Honesty is the foundation of recovery.

   - If you aren't honest with yourself and others, there's little chance you'll make it in this or any other treatment program.

   - Don't try to puff yourself up or make yourself into some kind of big shot.

   - Make it real and keep it that way.

2. **Let it all hang out.**

   - The most important thing that happens in group is self-disclosure.

   - Learn to be self-critical.

   - Opening up about your past, your feelings, your hopes, and your fears is the way you will uncover the thinking problems that get you in trouble over and over again.

   - The people who do not open up are not the tough guys—they're the ones who are most frightened. And they're also the ones most likely to keep ending up back behind bars.

   - Remember: you're only as sick as your secrets.

3. **Keep it confidential.**

   - What you hear in group stays in group. You are expected to maintain the highest level of confidentiality regarding all program participants.

If you aren't honest with yourself and others, there's little chance you'll make it in this or any other treatment program.

- Self-disclosure is about showing a bit of your soul to others in your community. This can be done only in a safe place—that means something discussed in group shouldn't end up all over the yard.

- If someone betrays your confidentiality, let it go: that's on the person who couldn't keep his mouth shut, not on you. If someone else isn't trustworthy, let him carry that burden. Don't you carry it.

4. **Keep an open mind.**

- Be willing to consider new viewpoints and to try different things. This is the only way you'll ever change, and recovery is about change.

- Think in new ways—get off automatic pilot.

- Don't let emotions run your life.

- Don't let others run your show by spending your time worrying about your "rep."

- Remember: your old thinking is what got you here. Why not try something new?

5. **Respect yourself.**

- No one can disrespect you as much as you've already disrespected yourself by putting yourself in this place, so if you think you're hot stuff, get over it.

- Expect to struggle early on, but work to move through those struggles; don't wallow in them.

- It's time you started to *really* respect yourself by believing that you can make it, that you can change, that you can have a better life.

- Stop listening to anyone who tries to bring you back down into the criminal and addictive life.

- Do your assignments thoroughly and on time—invest in yourself for once.

- Attend a self-help group (AA, NA, and so on) or other support activities on your own time.

6. **Respect your peers and the staff.**

  - Pick each other up and hold each other up—that's how a therapeutic community works.

  - Keep your peers accountable, and be grateful when they do the same for you. You may not like it, but they're trying to save your life. The least you can do is help them.

  - Speak to and treat staff with respect. They're trying to help you find a way to a better life.

  - Keep it positive. Negative attitudes undermine the treatment process for you and those around you.

  - Give up on the criminal code—it never works anyway. If there is BS going down, say so.

  - Don't swear.

7. **Respect your community.**

  - The men in your treatment unit are your family for now. Your loyalty is to helping them change, grow, recover.

  - Don't leave activities for any reason without permission of staff.

  - Keep yourself and your personal area clean.

8. **Hold yourself accountable.**

  - Don't make excuses.

  - Don't make out like you're the victim.

  - STOP WHINING.

  - Practice accepting criticism with grace.

- Realize that the things others say about you that make you the most angry are often the most on target. There's a lot you can learn from people you don't like.

- If you make a mistake, take responsibility, accept the consequences, and learn from it.

- Learn that being responsible for yourself is what being a real man is all about.

The Limits of Confidentiality

As we've discussed, confidentiality means that what you say in group must stay in group. It is one of the most important expectations of every group participant.

There are some exceptions and limits to this confidentiality. You need to know about them so you can make informed choices. These limits sometimes vary from state to state, so it is important that you discuss the limits of confidentiality with treatment staff in your correctional facility.

For example, it is almost certain that what you say in group or do on the unit *will be discussed* and tracked among *all* the therapists and supervisors in the program. While program staff members do not discuss treatment issues outside of the program, they will share such information with each other as they regularly discuss and evaluate your progress. That is a limit of confidentiality.

What you say in Group must stay in Group.

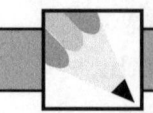

Confidentiality

Staff will now discuss with you what is and is not confidential in this program. Make a list of it all here so you can refer back to it as needed.

➤ What is confidential:

_____

_____

_____

_____

_____

_____

_____

➤ What is not confidential:

_____

_____

_____

_____

_____

_____

_____

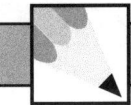

Living Unit and Institution Rules

➤ The expectations for your behavior and responsibilities in the living unit will be explained to you by staff at this time. Write them here so you can refer to them throughout this program.

Identification

_____

_____

_____

Count

_____

_____

_____

Movement

_____

_____

_____

Meals

_____

_____

_____

Cleanliness

_____

_____

_____

Clothing and property

_____

_____

_____

Work responsibilities

_____

_____

_____

Telephone use

_____

_____

_____

Noise

_____

_____

_____

Exercise, library, activities

_____

_____

_____

Chain of command (grievance procedures)

_____

_____

_____

Other important rules and regulations

_____

_____

_____

_____

_____

_____

_____

_____

While you are in this program, the therapeutic community will be your world. Your friends and "family" will be your peers. The community's rules and expectations are the ones you need to know and follow. If you do, change will come more easily. Don't waste your time fighting the rules, the staff, and your peers. If you do the work and practice the ideas in this program, a better life is yours for the taking.

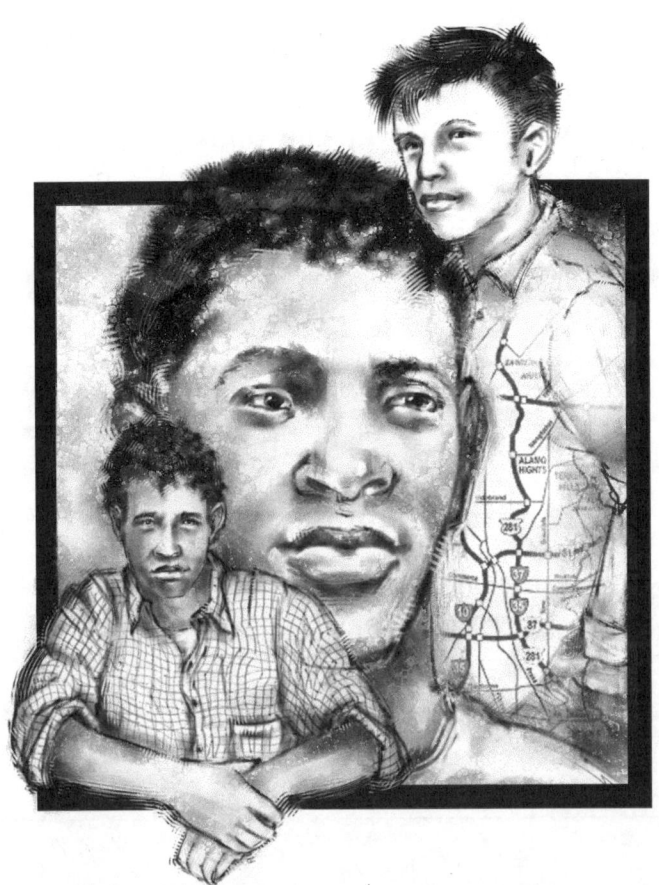

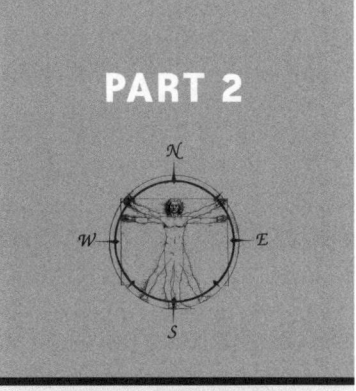

Introduction to Thinking about Your Thinking

Thinking is how we make sense of life. It gives meaning to events, our lives, and relationships. If we see a look on someone's face, thinking tells us what that look means. It tells us whether the person is happy, sad, angry, or annoyed. We might also hear a tone in someone's voice. Our thinking tells us what it means.

Based on what thinking tells us, we respond. If our thinking interprets someone's look as anger, we also get mad or just get out of the way. Our thinking directs us to do one thing rather than another. Thinking tells us how to cope with life.

EXERCISE 15 EXERCISE

Thinking about What You See

➤ Picture an expression that you saw on someone's face today. How would you describe the look?

_____

_____

_____

➤ What did your thinking tell you that the look meant?

_____

_____

_____

➤ What other interpretations or meanings might make sense?

_____

_____

_____

➤ Imagine yourself asking the person what the look meant. What might the person say? Try to think of several possible responses and list them below. What might be going on with the person to create that look? Indigestion? An upsetting phone call?

_____

_____

_____

_____

_____

■

Because we depend on our thinking to tell us what's going on, we like to believe that our thinking does a good job of guiding us. We like to believe that we've got things figured out, because that means we'll make it in the world. And it's true. Good thinking is a gold mine.

On the other hand, bad thinking is a dangerous, even deadly trap. Bad thinking creates holes we fall into and can't get out of. Thinking can be our best friend or our worst enemy.

Thinking about Thinking

Unfortunately, we usually don't pay attention to our thinking. We don't notice what we think, how we think, or how our thinking affects us. That's because thinking is invisible. It's all around us, influencing us constantly. Because it's not something we can touch, we don't see it.

Thinking is like wearing colored sunglasses. We get so used to them that we forget we have them on. Yet those glasses make everything look a certain way. If they're dark glasses, things appear darker than they are. If they're colored glasses, everything becomes that color. This means that if we think we're no good, we'll see everyone as treating us that way. Or if we think we're better than everyone else, we'll think it's okay to use or hurt others. If we think we're smart, we'll think we can get away with anything. Or if we think we have lots of willpower, we'll think we can stop our addiction anytime we want—that we're not really addicted.

EXERCISE **16** EXERCISE

Identifying "Thought Glasses"

We've seen how thinking is like wearing colored sunglasses. We see the world through our particular way of thinking; it's like we're looking at everything through "thought glasses." "Thought glasses" might be beliefs, assumptions, things we think we know. Take some time to think about some "thought glasses" you've noticed, either on yourself or on other people.

An example of "thought glasses" would be: "The world is a safe and happy place." (That's what is called "seeing the world through rose-colored glasses.") Another could be: "Life is supposed to be fair."

➤ List some of the "thought glasses" you've noticed, either on yourself or on other people.

_____

_____

_____

_____

➤ What was the thought (belief or assumption) behind these "thought glasses"?

_____

_____

➤ How does that thought make the world and other people look?

_____

_____

➤ How would a different thought make the world and other people look different?

_____

_____

Exercise 16 shows that there's more than one way to think—more than one pair of glasses to wear. It's easy to forget this. Since we're not inside anyone's head but our own, we assume our way of thinking is the only way to think. We think it's the way everyone thinks. And when we think something about a person or situation, we think that's the way it is—that there's no other way to see it. Yet this is just not true. Our minds can wear all kinds of glasses and so see the world in many different ways.

Thinking is powerful, for better or for worse. It can help you create a happy life. It can land you behind bars and leave you there. It can make you feel like a loser. It can give you hope that you can change. Thinking can make change happen. It can change *you*.

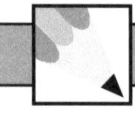

EXERCISE 17 EXERCISE

Think about Your Thinking

Think about your relationship to your thinking and how your thinking has affected you.

➤ When has my thinking helped me?

_____

_____

➤ When has it gotten me in trouble?

_____

_____

"There is nothing either good or bad, but thinking makes it so."

— Shakespeare

➤ Have I ever changed my thinking? If yes, how?

_____

_____

➤ Have I ever seen someone else change their thinking?
If yes, how?

_____

_____

➤ How did a change in thinking make me see things
differently?

_____

_____

You're in this program to learn how to make thinking
your best friend. It's a helper that is always there for you.
The treasure of thinking can be yours. It's not magic. It just
takes some training. Many people before you have gone
through this program and discovered the power of their own
thinking. They've learned to turn their own thinking into a
powerful partner rather than a personal stumbling block.

Your Mental Map

To start, you need to learn some basics about thinking. Your thinking serves you like a map. It's a map that your mind uses to get around. When you're in a new place, you need a good map. Not just any map will do. You need a map that fits the world you're in. And you need a map that tells you what you need to know. A map that shows underground water levels or weather patterns won't help you get from your unit to the mess hall.

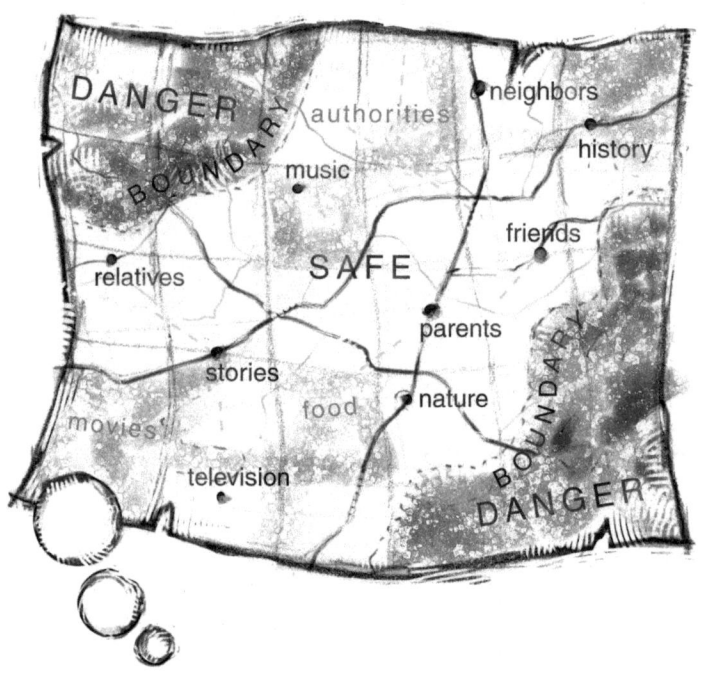

As a map of life, our mental map has a big job. That's because we need to know a lot. We need to know how to have good relationships at home and at work. We need to know how to work. Many of us need to know how to raise children. Since we're confronted with new information all the time, we need to know how to learn. When we feel pain, we need to know how to deal with it and heal. And we need to know how to take care of ourselves. This is one of the biggest jobs we have that affects all the others.

Your Mental Map

➤ In the space below, make a list of all the areas of your life that you need your mental map for. What parts of living require you to think? This will include just about every part of your life except sleeping and being drunk or high. For example, you rely on your mental map to fill out this workbook. You rely on it to get you to lunch.

_____

_____

_____

_____

_____

_____

_____

_____

_____

_____

_____

_____

51

It's not that we don't have a mental map already. You do. We all do. We create our map as we're growing up. From the day we're born, we're continually drawing our mental map. The map helps us make sense of people, experiences, relationships, and our place in life. In fact, everything that we do helps to form our mental map.

Our map is never finished. It's changing all the time. One reason is that we change. This means our *needs* change. The map we used when we were five years old isn't enough for us now. We have different experiences now. We need a map that helps us cope with them.

Another reason maps change is that they never tell the whole story. They're only a version of reality. The maps that our minds use have their limits. It's important that we know about those limits.

We need a mental map. We can't get around without one. We need some concept in our heads about what's going on, or we're lost. But we also need to know that our map can mislead us. Maps get old. When our lives change and our map stays the same, we get lost. Things no longer make sense. We don't know what to do, or we do the wrong thing that may hurt others and ourselves. A faulty map can lead us to interpret events in ways that lead to trouble.

With a faulty map, the pathway to paradise can turn out to be the road to ruin.

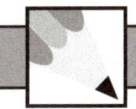

Using a Faulty Map

Think about a time when your mental map got you in trouble, when what you assumed or believed about reality led you into a bad situation. For example, you may have believed that another criminal wouldn't snitch on you because of the criminal code, but he did anyway. Or you may have been sure you'd never get caught for your crime—until you did.

➤ What was the situation?

_____

_____

_____

➤ What mental map were you using?

_____

_____

_____

➤ Do you still use that map? (check one)

_____ Yes   _____ No

If you do, would you consider changing it? Why or why not?

_____

_____

➤ If you have changed that mental map, what is your new map for a similar situation?

_____

_____

_____

_____

_____

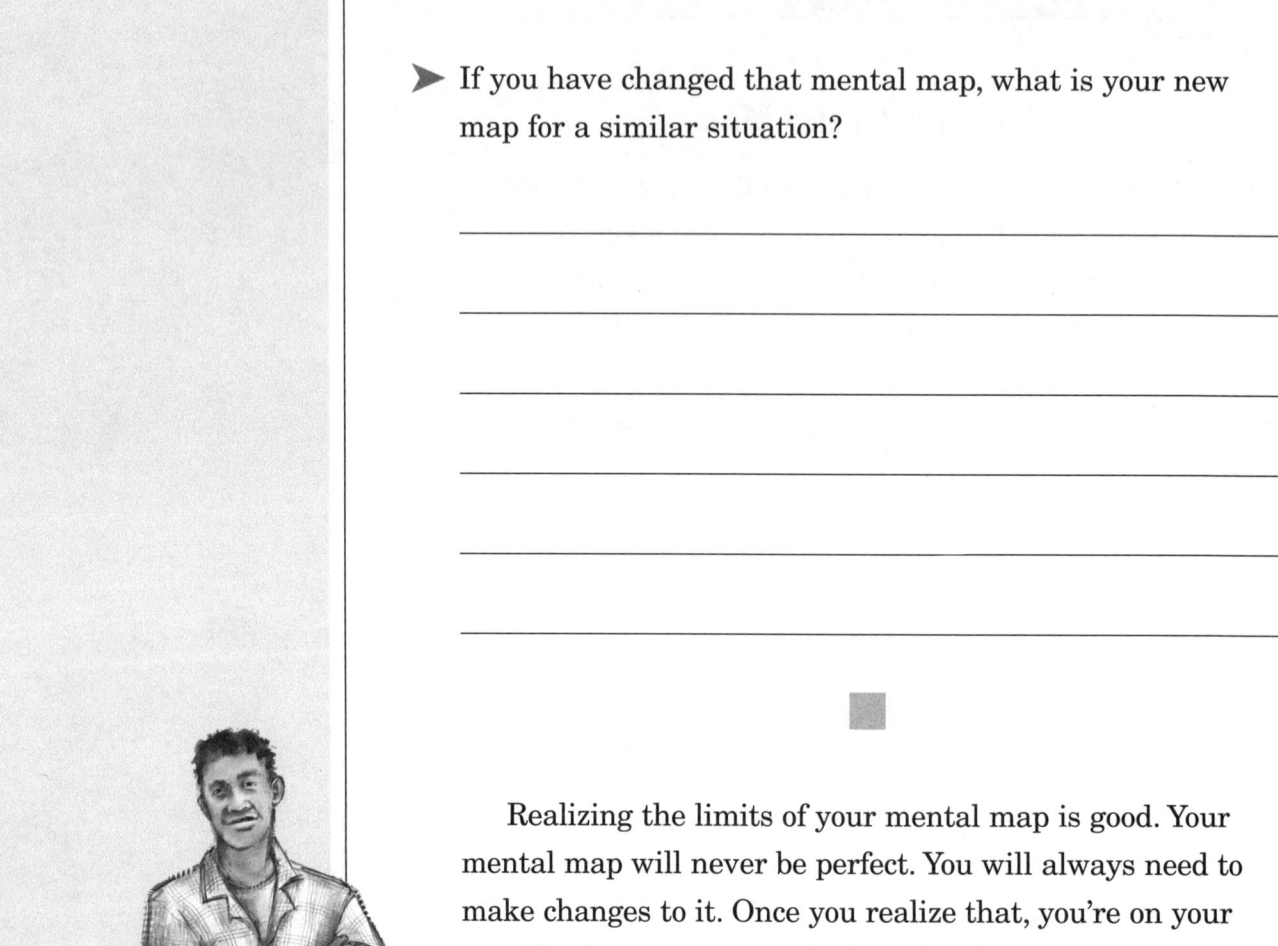

Realizing the limits of your mental map is good. Your mental map will never be perfect. You will always need to make changes to it. Once you realize that, you're on your way. You know your map is there. You know you need it to get around. And you know you can change it.

This program is designed to show you how to change your mental map so that it works for you as you change. Learning about your mental map will change you, and you will change it as you go along. It's a two-way process that takes you down a new road in a new direction.

"The beginning of wisdom is knowing that you don't know."

— Socrates, philosopher

Thinking and Behavior

You can't see thinking. It's something you do that is invisible. But its effects are powerful. Two people may face the same situation, but they may respond in opposite ways. One person may end up hurting someone. The other may save someone's life. The difference is in how they think—the mental maps they use to guide their actions.

Your job here is to become aware of your thinking. You will learn to observe your thoughts and notice your thought patterns. This is a skill you need now and for the rest of your life. It's not easy, though. Like many people, you never learned to think about your thinking. You assume that what you think is "just the way things are." You've been using your map as if it's the only map there is. It's not. When something happens that makes you mad, you react. You don't notice how thinking comes into the process.

EXERCISE **20** EXERCISE

Did You Have a Choice?

Think about a time when you thought you had no choice about how to act. It could be a recent experience such as something you said or did to somebody while incarcerated. It could be related to when you committed a crime. It should be a situation where you really felt at the time that there was no other alternative but to do what you did.

➤ What was the situation?

_____

_____

_____

➤ What thoughts were going through your mind?

_____

_____

_____

➤ Looking back at the situation now, how could you have acted differently? How might someone else have reacted?

_____

_____

_____

■

To get out of the mess you're in and to start behaving differently, you need to stop looking *through* your mental map and start looking *at* it. Otherwise, your mind is locked up inside a faulty map. That's how you got locked up in the first place. Your mind's map guides you. If you have a bad map, you're going to go from one bad experience to another. You'll behave like a complete jerk and think you have no other choice. You do have a choice. Understanding how your thinking works gives you that choice. Thinking about thinking and observing your mental map give you options you didn't know you had. Noticing your thoughts gives you options for living that you didn't think you had.

How Does Thinking Work?

Thoughts arise in response to events. A man cuts in front of you in line. Immediately, your mind pulls out your mental map. "What a selfish son of a b——! He deserves to be put in his place!" With that mental map, you shout at or maybe even hit the man. The event called up your mental map. This gave you specific thoughts about how to handle the situation. Then you acted. You did exactly what your mental map told you to do. Figure 1 shows how this works.

Figure 1

The event leads to the thoughts. The thoughts cause the behavior.

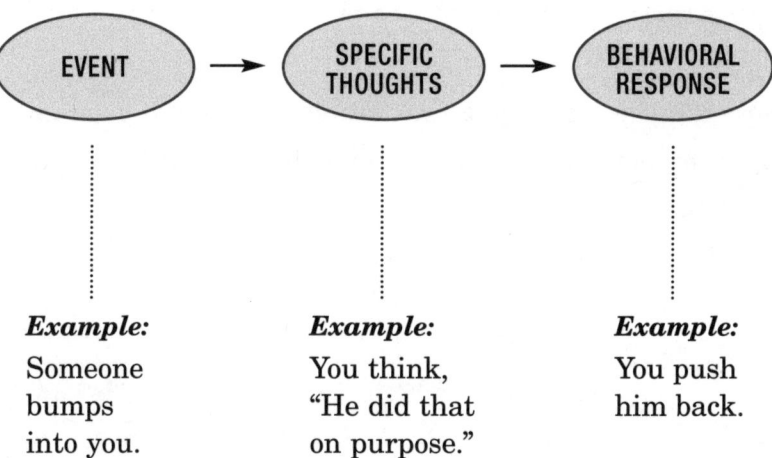

Example:
Someone bumps into you.

Example:
You think, "He did that on purpose."

Example:
You push him back.

This usually happens so fast that you don't notice all the pieces of the process. Something happens, wham, you react. Knee-jerk. Automatic. Yes, that's exactly how it seems, because you're so used to obeying your map. Until you understand how your thoughts work and where you get them, you become their puppet.

To get your life back, you need to get wise to your thinking. Your behaviors are *always* the result of your thinking, whether you realize it or not. What goes on in your brain calls the shots, and your behavior *never* bypasses your brain.

Looking at Automatic Behavior

➤ Describe something you did that was automatic, immediate, as if no thoughts were involved. This will be a situation where something happened, and you reacted right away. It could be a recent experience or a situation from before you were incarcerated.

_____

_____

➤ Now run the memory of that situation through your mind again in slow motion. Do it slowly enough that you can recall some of the thoughts that were swirling around in your head. What thoughts do you remember?

_____

_____

➤ Why did those thoughts make you behave as you did?

_____

_____

➤ Given those thoughts, did your actions make sense? Why or why not?

_____

_____

➤ How could you have thought differently? What different thoughts would make you react differently to the same situation?

_____

_____

_____

_____

■

We're going to work on helping you learn to notice your thoughts. The goal is for this to become automatic for you. After you get good at this, you can think about whether the mental map you're using is the one that works best for you. Are you going to be controlled by a mental map that puts you back behind bars? Or are you going to make the choice to change your map, to think different, positive thoughts? Before we get into reporting on your thoughts, you need to understand how your feelings come into play.

Thinking and Feelings

Feelings: they come on us like waves and sweep us away. They seem far more powerful than mere thoughts. Feelings drown you and assume a life of their own. Feelings take you over, and you feel powerless to stop them. When they pass, especially the negative, destructive feelings, you look at what you did in the grip of anger or rage and feel bad. Or maybe you don't. Maybe you feel you had every right to feel and act as you did, and you'd feel and act the same way again.

Feelings take you over, and you feel powerless to stop them.

Thinking about Feelings, Part 1

➤ Think about the feelings you've experienced over the last twenty-four hours. What feelings did you experience most strongly?

_____

_____

_____

➤ Do you think you had a choice in feeling that way? (check one)

_____ Yes   _____ No

Why or why not?

_____

_____

Feelings are powerful. But like mental maps, they can be cruel masters. They can destroy your life and happiness. What you don't realize is that your powerful feelings are servants of your thoughts. You can learn to choose what feelings you have and where they take you. This choice comes from choosing your thoughts, your mental map.

Pretend you are a huge jet plane. The passengers are the people and events that fill your life. The massive engines are your feelings. But what guides the plane? What determines its direction? The pilot, who sits hidden away in the cockpit.

Compared with the size of the plane, the human pilot is small. What guides the pilot is his or her brain, which is even smaller. In terms of size, the pilot seems insignificant and invisible. In truth, he or she is in charge.

The pilot of your plane, the one who turns on the engines of your feelings and sends them off in one direction or another, is your thoughts, your mental map. Your feelings make loud roaring noises. You experience their raw power. But your thoughts direct them. Your mental map gives your feelings direction, for better or for worse.

Not all thoughts direct your feelings well. Thoughts can behave like terrorists, taking over your plane and destroying you and everyone around you. When terroristic thoughts take over the plane, the powerful jet engines became forces for destruction. Thoughts seem tiny and powerless, but they can be deadly. Raw power isn't the issue. What matters is what directs that power—what directs the power of your feelings and behavior—and that's what your thoughts do.

Figure 2

Feelings also result from thoughts.

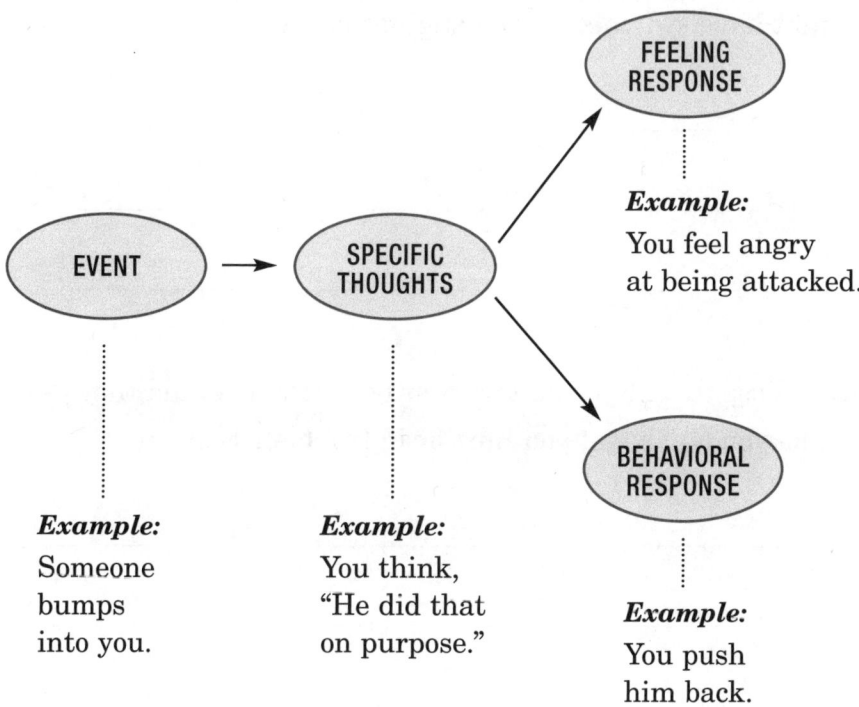

Example:
You feel angry at being attacked.

EVENT → SPECIFIC THOUGHTS

Example:
Someone bumps into you.

Example:
You think, "He did that on purpose."

BEHAVIORAL RESPONSE

Example:
You push him back.

Your behaviors and your feelings are always the result of your thinking, whether you experience it that way or not. Feelings do not result from events. Thoughts come in between, directing you to feel one way or another about an event.

 EXERCISE **23** EXERCISE

Thinking about Feelings, Part 2

➤ In the space below, describe some of the powerful feelings you've had since you've been incarcerated.

_____

_____

_____

➤ Now go into slow motion, and try to identify the thoughts that come to you around those feelings. Which thoughts might have switched on the engines of these feelings?

_____

_____

_____

➤ Did those thoughts lead to a positive outcome or did they make you crash (get you hurt or in trouble)? Explain.

_____

_____

_____

_____

_____

➤ Imagine other thoughts that might have made you feel differently. List those thoughts here and describe how they might have made you feel.

_____

_____

_____

_____

_____

➤ What different actions might have resulted from those thoughts?

_____

_____

_____

_____

_____

Your behaviors and your feelings are always the result of your thinking.

You can learn to choose what feelings you have and where they take you.

Introduction to Thinking Reports

Some event happens, and thoughts flood in. They come directly from the mental map you've developed over the course of your life. You probably couldn't name all the parts of your mental map. You probably can't even name all the thoughts flashing through your mind to tell you how to deal with an event, especially a threatening one. Your mind has been moving fast. When you acted on the resulting thoughts in the past, you ended up here incarcerated. It's time you understood what's going on in your head, because that's the place to start turning your life around.

Your mind may seem wild and confusing to you, but it actually operates in patterns. When you think the same thoughts over and over, you create habits of thinking. These habits form thinking patterns: "Life is supposed to be fair, and it's not." "The toughest survive." "Do it to others before they do it to you." "I'm looking out for number one." "Just don't get in my way." "See if I care!" "To hell with you!" Such negative thinking patterns, as well as positive ones, create your mind's geography.

Thinking patterns become so familiar to you that you can't imagine thinking any other way. You believe that your way of thinking reflects both reality—"That's just the way it is"—and who you are—"That's just the way I am."

But these thinking patterns are your real prisons, the mind-prisons that got you here.

Your thinking patterns trap you, and they'll trap you again and again, until you change your mental patterns.

Habits of Thinking

➤ Sit back for a moment and recall your thinking habits. What thoughts occur to you over and over?

_____

_____

_____

➤ What words or phrases keep running through your head?

_____

_____

_____

➤ What do you hear yourself saying to people a lot?

_____

_____

_____

➤ What story do you use to make sense of life?

_____

_____

_____

You create your patterns of thinking over time. They're learned mental habits. You aren't born with them. You can unlearn what has made you self-destructive. You can take apart your patterns and put them together again in new ways. This is your challenge.

To change your thinking patterns, you need to know what they are. To start with, you are going to fill out Thinking Reports. Think of these reports as photographs of your thinking processes. Over time, you can compare the photographs and see patterns that will help you make changes.

When people report something, they try (or should try) to be as accurate as possible. That's because we all need accurate information to decide what to do next. Right now, you need to know precisely what's going on in your mental processes in order to change them. You only hurt yourself by making things up, exaggerating, saying what you think someone wants to hear, or lying about what's happened, what you're thinking, or what you did. If you are dishonest, you'll stay a puppet of your feelings. You'll be a victim of your mental map that hijacks your life and brings you trouble. In other words, you'll stay stuck in the thinking habits that got you here. You have a choice. Either be honest with yourself, or hang on to your mental map that put you behind bars.

We suggest you make your Thinking Reports as simple, straightforward, and accurate as possible. Then they can help you. Eventually, you'll become aware of your own thinking. You'll get into the habit of observing your own thoughts. And then you'll be able to start thinking about your thinking. You'll compare these snapshots of your mental map and find out why your mental map led you behind bars. Then you can use this awareness to create a new, more successful mental map.

To identify your thinking process, you need to report on four things:

1. The **Event**—what exactly happened to begin the chain of thoughts, feelings, and behaviors.

2. Your **Thoughts**—what popped into your mind when the event occurred.

3. Your **Feelings**—the emotions or other sensations that resulted from your thoughts about the event.

4. Your **Behavior**—your actions in response to the event that your thoughts directed you to do and your feelings pushed you to do.

Report the Event

What happened? You want to give the newspaper version—"just the facts." You want to state the "who, what, where, and when" of the situation as completely as you can. You may find it easier to imagine telling the story of the event as if you were someone else watching it—a bystander. Don't include more than you know. You don't know about other people's intentions, why they did what they did. You probably have your own opinions and judgments about the event. Don't include them. They're not facts. Leave out your feelings, too. This isn't the place to express them, not yet. We'll come to that later.

who, what
where, when

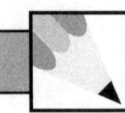

Reporting an Event

➤ Think of an interaction you had with another person in the past week. It can be about anything. You are just practicing being an accurate reporter of your own life, so write a report of what happened—"just the facts."

_____

_____

_____

_____

_____

_____

_____

_____

_____

_____

_____

_____

■

Report Your Thoughts

Thoughts pop into your head when the event occurs. They are your mind's automatic responses. Usually, you don't sit down and reason things out. Rather, thoughts start coming into your mind almost on their own.

EXERCISE **26** EXERCISE

Reporting Thoughts

➤ Review the event you used in exercise 25. Then, write a report of what thoughts popped into your head at that time. You may have had one thought or several. List whatever you can remember.

_____

_____

_____

_____

_____

_____

_____

_____

_____

Report Your Feelings

Emotions will also come up at the time of an event. These emotions may be sadness, anxiety, anger, pleasure, relief, fear, or other feelings. You probably experience these feelings as being separate from the automatic thoughts you had. But that's not so. Your thought patterns set you up to have those feelings. As long as you keep certain thinking habits, certain feelings will follow. That's why you need to be specific when you report your feelings, not only identifying your feelings, but also the intensity of them. The more accurate you are in naming your feelings and describing them, the more you'll be able to see how they come from your thoughts.

EXERCISE **27** EXERCISE

Reporting Feelings

➤ Review the event you described in exercise 25 again. This time, as you recall your thoughts, notice what feelings come up, and write a report about them. Name the feelings and then describe them—mild, fairly intense, very intense, or overwhelming.

_____

_____

_____

_____

_____

_____

Report Your Behavior

What you say or do in response to the event makes up your behavior. It is the direct result of the automatic thoughts. Your action results from your thinking. Your mouth and body can't move unless your brain tells them to. Your brain operates through thought. Often your actions will use a criminal or addictive tactic. This is a strategy you have learned to use to try to get the results you think you want. Here again, your report of your behavior should be as straightforward and accurate as possible. You should limit it to what you actually did and only that. Don't put in what you hope or believe the effect of your action might have been, such as teaching someone a lesson. Just describe your behavior—exactly what you did or said.

EXERCISE 28 EXERCISE

Reporting Behavior

➤ Review the event you described in exercise 25 again. Then, report on what you said or did in response to your thoughts.

_____

_____

_____

_____

_____

_____

_____

The more you fill out Thinking Reports, the sooner you'll learn to observe your thoughts and be able to think about your thinking. Try to do one report every day. You need the exercise. As with building muscles, you have to keep at it every day.

And when you don't feel like doing it, remember what's at stake. To take charge of your plane and not crash, you've got to know how to pilot. Your mental map has been destructive to others and to you. We just call it by another name: criminal and addictive thinking.

Introduction to Criminal Thinking

You are behind bars for a reason. It's not because you're no good, worthless, or useless to society. Each person has worth and value, including you. But destructive habits of thought can destroy your value. Because you're here, chances are you have thinking habits similar to most criminals and addicts. You may have picked up these habits from many people and hard experiences. We're here to help you change those habits, no matter where they came from. You can then claim your worth as a human being and express it to yourself and others.

Every human brain holds immense power and knowledge, including yours. It's much more powerful than the most advanced computer. But our brains didn't come with instruction manuals. We don't know how to use them. Even the smartest humans use only 3 to 4 percent of their brain's power.

Criminals and addicts like you use ways of thinking that make the brain function destructively, to themselves and others. *How* you think is distorted. You have behavior problems because you *first* have thinking problems. You will learn more about this later. Because you have distorted habits of thinking, what you think is also distorted, confused, and destructive. Your thinking habits make it very hard for you to reason clearly and draw good conclusions. Your mind doesn't work right because of faulty mental habits. The good news is that you can change these patterns.

Criminal thinking patterns are types of thoughts that say it is okay to violate others or their property. We describe several of these patterns as "stances."

Stances are like masks or costumes.

When you feel empty and worthless inside, you adopt a stance. When you feel bigger and better than others, you adopt a stance. You do this to look good, strong, tough, or whatever you think you need or deserve. But the stances aren't you. They don't come from inside. They're fake. You think you need your stances because you feel like nothing without them. You've probably used them since you were a child, when you were helpless and vulnerable. But you're no longer a child, and they're not working for you now.

There are nine criminal thinking patterns. You'll learn more about them later in the *Criminal & Addictive Thinking* module. We're just giving you a brief introduction to them now.

1. **Victim Stance.** Anytime you find yourself blaming anyone or anything for what you have done, you are thinking from a victim stance. Anytime you make excuses for violating people or their property, you're using a victim stance.

2. **"Good Person" Stance.** When you ignore the harm you're doing to others by claiming that you're a good person, you use this stance. You are not separate from your actions. If you act hurtfully, you are not acting like a good person. Telling yourself that you are is self-deception, no matter what other good deeds you may do. All the good you do is no excuse for harming others.

You think no one in the whole world is like you or has experienced what you have.

3. **"Unique Person" Stance.** You think no one in the whole world is like you or has experienced what you have. Because you're in a class of your own, rules that apply to others don't apply to you. You think you're smarter, better, and are in a position to judge and condemn others. Other people make mistakes and learn from them. You don't. You see yourself as living above everyone else and the law. You lack compassion for others— and for yourself, actually.

4. **Fear of Exposure.** As a criminal thinker, you deal in fear. You like others to think you're fearless. But you are consumed with fears. You fear that you are nobody and worthless, that you will be found out, and above all, that you'll be exposed as someone vulnerable and full of fear. So you adopt a stance of invincibility. You don't trust anyone. You don't let anyone get close to you. You act like you know everything. You want to prove how powerful you are by hurting someone and getting away with it.

5. **Lack-of-Time Perspective.** Most criminal thinkers do not have a good understanding of time. You don't learn from the past, and you don't think about future consequences. You see your behavior as isolated. You want instant gratification, so you act on the spur of the moment. You want all the rewards of life, but you don't want to have to work for them. You're not willing to put in the long-term effort that worthwhile goals require.

6. **Selective Effort.** Effort is a sincere, sustained, consistent attempt to exert yourself mentally and/or physically to achieve a goal. As a criminal thinker, you use selective effort but don't use it to

achieve responsible goals. You go for the quick fix, the easy bucks, the scam. You think you deserve to get something without earning it or working for it like everyone else must do.

7. **Use of Power to Control.** As a criminal thinker, you use this to get your way. But the power you use is not real, authentic power. It's not based on knowledge, discipline, self-control, and self-awareness. It's fake power. It is used to manipulate, intimidate, humiliate, and dominate others. It helps you get what you want or avoid feeling worthless and vulnerable. You put yourself up by putting others down. It inspires no true respect, only distance in relationships.

8. **Seek Excitement First.** This pattern makes you avoid responsible behavior. Yet responsible behavior brings excitement, too, and far more meaning and fulfillment. But it does take effort. Effort is not something you understand. Instead, you've fallen into a pattern of getting bored easily. You don't like to be alone for very long or to stick with a task. You take adrenaline-pumping risks. It's easy to see how this leads to criminal behavior.

9. **Ownership Stance.** This pattern shows a distorted view of your boundaries: what's yours and what's not. You think everything is yours or at least that you have the right to get it from others by any means. You also think people are property that you can possess and do with whatever you want. You can yell at them, shame them, hit them, rape them, rob them, or kill them. You don't realize that other people are equal human beings, separate from you and with their own rights and property you must respect.

These nine criminal thinking patterns present a clear picture of the mental map that has led you and anyone else who thinks in these ways to pain and incarceration. You're here to change them.

EXERCISE 29 EXERCISE

Your Criminal Thinking Patterns

➤ Review the nine criminal thinking patterns. Which three jump out at you as patterns you see yourself using regularly?

1. _____

2. _____

3. _____

➤ Describe an incident that shows how you think in a criminal thinking pattern.

_____

_____

_____

Here are the nine **criminal thinking patterns**:

- victim stance
- "good person" stance
- "unique person" stance
- fear of exposure
- lack-of-time perspective
- selective effort
- use of power to control
- seek excitement first
- ownership stance

Criminal thinking patterns are types of thoughts that say it is okay to violate others or their property.

Introduction to Addictive Thinking

Addictive thinking patterns are very similar to criminal thinking patterns. Criminal thinking patterns say it is okay to violate others or their property. *Addictive thinking patterns* say it is okay to use alcohol or other drugs as much as you want and to do whatever you need to do to get them.

The main feature of addictive thinking is *denial*. Denial is a trick the addict's mind plays to excuse the use of alcohol and other drugs no matter what harm it causes. You can see how others are heading down a self-destructive road through addiction, but you can't seem to see this in yourself. If you really saw this, you'd have to begin your recovery. You avoid this truth in order to keep using.

You keep using because you're obsessed with the desire to feel good. You don't feel good without consuming an addictive substance (alcohol or other drugs, food, nicotine) or engaging in an addictive process (sex, gambling, dominating, raging). So, your mind becomes obsessed with repeating the experience. You're so absorbed in your own cravings that you are unable to consider the wants and needs of others. You become *self-obsessed*.

Obsessed with addictive cravings, you can't think straight. You *think irrationally,* because your thoughts revolve around justifying and excusing your addiction. You're not open to the truth. To stay in denial, you lie, invent stories, twist facts—anything that serves your addiction.

The main feature of addictive thinking is denial.

Denial, self-obsession, and irrational thinking are the characteristics of addictive thinking. What thinking patterns are involved? Basically, the same patterns as for criminal thinking except they're focused on keeping addictive rather than criminal behaviors going.

1. **Self-Pity Stance.** As with the victim stance of criminal thinking, the self-pity stance makes you think that you are a victim of circumstances beyond your control. You're down on your luck, and you think the world is out to get you. As a result, you have a hard time taking responsibility for what happens to you. "Poor me . . . I can't help it."

2. **"Good Person" Stance.** This stance allows you to overlook all the damage you're doing to yourself and others. You selectively remember only the good things you've done. You conveniently forget all the ways your use of alcohol or other drugs has messed up your life and hurt the people you care about most. This stance feeds your denial about the price you're paying for remaining addicted.

3. **"Unique Person" Stance.** For the addict, this stance is as seductive and destructive as it is for the criminal. You think you're different and special in a way that puts you above everyone else. You think the destructive nature of addiction doesn't apply to you. You probably have lots of stories about your mysterious, tragic, or adventurous life. You want to make your addiction seem attractive and exciting. Putting yourself above everyone, you think you're always right and can tell people what their problems are. You use your mind to argue and bully people to prove how much better you are.

4. **Fear of Exposure.** As an addict, you don't want to stop using. You're afraid to do this. You're afraid of confronting yourself and your real situation, because then you'd have to change. You'd have to come to terms with your real worth as a human being. Instead of doing that, you run to people who support your addiction and avoid those who don't. You even take pride in your substance abuse. At the same time, you're haunted by the belief that you're worthless, a nobody, and empty inside. You're most afraid of exposing yourself.

5. **Lack-of-Time Perspective.** When all that's on your mind is your next drink or next fix, you don't think about your using history and what it has cost you. You don't think about the consequences of your using in the future. The past, present, and future don't exist. Because of this thinking, you don't see cause and effect clearly. When people get upset with you because of your addiction, you resent them and think they're treating you unfairly. You don't realize that their reactions result from your addictive behavior. You're out of touch with reality.

6. **Selective Effort.** You have plenty of energy and drive to keep the addiction going but not enough for day-to-day obligations and responsibilities. You and your addiction get all your energy. You think somehow everything else will magically take care of itself, if only you can keep using. You're not thinking about completing your education or getting a job. They're too boring. Rather, you seek out people who will take care of you and enable you to stay addicted.

7. **Use of Deceit to Control.** As an addict, you lie. You lie to yourself through denial about your addiction. And you lie to others, using deceit, half-truths, omitted truths, and outright lies to keep others from challenging your addiction. Through deceit, you control others. It's a power tactic. As long as it looks like you're in control, you'll be able to keep using. You become defensive when people challenge you about your chemical use. You argue because you think you must always be right about everything. The more you do this, the more you're out of touch with reality—and out of control.

8. **Seek Pleasure First.** As an addictive thinker, you seek pleasure first. You'll sacrifice your health, relationships, family, freedom, reputation in your community—everything—to get the momentary pleasure of being high. You can't tolerate being uncomfortable. You want to relieve it as soon as possible by using. But it doesn't work that way. Your body builds up a tolerance to whatever substance you're using. So, each time you feel less and less pleasure from it. Misery results. Your denial becomes stronger to keep your addiction going.

9. **Ownership Stance.** As with criminal thinking patterns, addictive thinking patterns fail to recognize healthy boundaries. In fact, your boundaries are one-way: "What's mine is mine, and what's yours is mine." Your obsession with using makes you disregard the property rights of others. You believe it's okay for you to steal from others or to cheat them, so you can get what you want. This stance makes you feel you're entitled to get whatever you want by whatever means— that you're above the law.

Your Addictive Thinking Patterns

➤ Review the nine addictive thinking patterns. Which three patterns do you see yourself falling into regularly?

1. _____

2. _____

3. _____

➤ Describe an incident that shows how you think in an addictive thinking pattern.

_____

_____

_____

Here are the nine
addictive thinking patterns:

- self-pity stance
- "good person" stance
- "unique person" stance
- fear of exposure
- lack-of-time perspective
- selective effort
- use of deceit to control
- seek pleasure first
- ownership stance

Addictive thinking patterns say it is okay to use alcohol or other drugs as much as you want and to do whatever you need to do to get them.

Anyone using criminal and addictive thinking patterns is going to behave in destructive ways that may lead to incarceration. Correcting the behavior starts with correcting the thinking.

Introduction to Criminal and Addictive Tactics

Behavior is the result of your thinking. Criminal and addictive behavior is the result of criminal and addictive thinking. Your habits of mind have created your habits of acting. And they *are* habits. You use them over and over, because you think they work well for you. Manipulating, deceiving, intimidating, controlling, and violating others has become second nature. These are your tactics, your ways of coping with people and situations. For you, criminal and addictive tactics have become your way of surviving.

The use of criminal and addictive tactics is a habit of behavior you will have to change in order to recover from both your criminal behavior and your addiction. To change these habits and recover, you need to understand the thinking behind the tactics—why you do what you do.

Tactics are planned strategies and approaches designed to achieve a goal. Everyone uses tactics of some sort. People use responsible tactics to plan behaviors that accomplish something helpful and worthwhile for them, their families, and their communities. People use irresponsible tactics to try to get the most by giving the least. These tactics hide their motives. This means taking advantage of others, avoiding responsibility, and causing hurt for selfish gain.

Criminal and addictive tactics are divided into three types of strategies:

1. avoidance strategies

2. diversion strategies

3. aggression strategies

You will need to learn to recognize when you are using these strategies. Being aware that you're using them is the first step toward changing them. Each type of tactic or strategy takes many forms.

Your habits of mind have created your habits of acting.

Avoidance Strategies

There are many ways to avoid responsibility for your actions and to get away with behaving irresponsibly.

- Lying is the most obvious tactic, and it takes many forms. You might tell a complete lie, or you might tell half-truths, omitting information that you know is important.

- You can be deliberately vague, pretending you don't know things or can't remember them.

- You might stay silent to avoid notice. With counselors, you might pretend that you're going along with treatment, when you really have no intention of taking any of it seriously or of changing yourself.

- You might do the minimum to get by without showing any real commitment to change.

- You might also play dumb, like you're too "out of it" to understand the treatment work.

Not making the choice to learn shows that you are avoiding the central issues of your life.

EXERCISE **31** EXERCISE

How Do You Avoid Responsibility?

➤ What specific avoidance tactics do you use to get yourself off the hook? How do you avoid work or accountability? What are your "secrets" for keeping a low profile so you won't be noticed?

_____

_____

_____

_____

_____

_____

➤ Describe the last time you used an avoidance strategy.

_____

_____

_____

_____

■

Diversion Strategies

When some form of lying doesn't work, you try to shift the focus off you and onto someone or something else. You try to confuse people or direct their attention away from you, off the real issues. For example, you throw your energy into pointing out the faults and failures of others. You magnify or exaggerate minor issues just to stir the pot and muddy the waters. You might even deliberately try to confuse others so you can get the upper hand.

Telling inconsistent versions of an event, jumping around from point to point, speaking either too quickly or too slowly, or using slang or double-talk that others don't understand are all ways of confusing people. If all else fails, you shame yourself publicly, hoping that people will feel sorry for you and not hold you accountable for your conduct.

How Do You Divert Attention?

➤ What specific tactics do you use to take the focus off your uncomfortable issues?

_____

_____

➤ How do you get others thinking about someone or something other than holding you responsible for your behaviors?

_____

_____

➤ How do you divert attention away from yourself?

_____

_____

➤ Describe the last time you used a diversion strategy.

_____

_____

_____

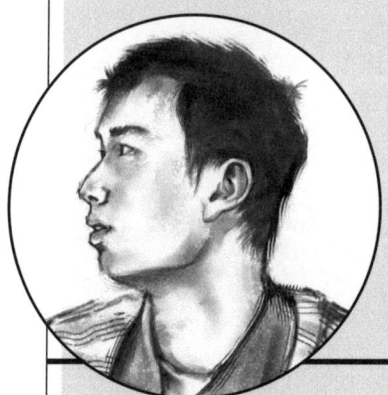

You try to confuse people or direct their attention away from you, off the real issues.

Aggression Strategies

When avoiding responsibility or diverting attention doesn't work, you try something different. You use tactics of aggression: attacking, intimidating, stirring up conflict, or instilling fear in others by threatening them. If caught, you take on the victim role, claiming that you were provoked or that the other person deserved it. Arguing is where aggression tactics start. Sarcasm and mean-spirited teasing set the stage for bad feelings. This is when arguments break out. Arguing turns a chance for communication into a power struggle with attacks and threats. From there it can lead to violence.

In treatment programs, you use aggression strategies when you try to split the staff members by pitting one against another. You also try to split groups, because then it's easier to create chaos and conflict. You try to create a world that's familiar to you and that you think you know how to control, instead of working to change yourself. With aggression tactics, your goal is to get what you want, to escape exposure, and above all, to avoid confronting your inner emptiness ("zero state") by keeping others on the defensive.

How Do You Use Aggression Tactics?

➤ What specific tactics do you use to intimidate, threaten, or bully others?

_____

_____

_____

_____

➤ Describe the last time you used an aggression strategy.

_____

_____

_____

_____

As a criminal and addictive thinker, you cannot make progress in treatment until you give up using these criminal and addictive tactics. Again, being aware of how you're behaving and why you're behaving that way is how you can start changing your habits.

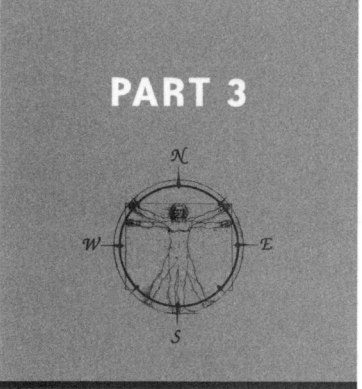

PART 3

A NEW DIRECTION

A Cognitive-Behavioral Treatment Curriculum

Introduction to Addiction and Recovery

All addicts get to a point where they know something is wrong—that their lives are a mess. Addiction is like a tornado, tearing through your life destroying everything in its path. All of your relationships suffer: with your family, friends, community, and, most of all, your relationship with yourself. All are severely damaged by addiction.

Addicts and Addiction: How Addiction Works

The trouble with addiction is that you don't see it coming until it's too late. You're caught in the addiction tornado and can't get out. If it were easy to stop, though, it wouldn't be addiction. Addiction is a disease. Your body and brain are now addicted to a chemical substance. The fact that you haven't been able to stop doesn't mean you are weak, bad, stupid, or immoral. It means you have the disease of addiction.

It is the only disease where those with it firmly deny that they have it. In their "self-talk," addicts typically say, "I don't need help," "I don't use that much," "I can quit any-time; I just don't want to yet," or "I don't have a problem." Denial is one of the greatest hurdles to treatment and recovery. You're not motivated to fix something if you truly believe there's nothing wrong. That's how the disease of addiction continues untreated. Addiction is a progressive, confusing, fatal disease. You'll die if you stay addicted.

Instead of confronting your deadly disease, you make excuses for keeping your use going. You might say, "I had a tough childhood, so what do people expect?" "Just this once, and I won't use again," "It's my life; I'll do what I want," or "I don't hurt anyone when I use." You scam yourself to keep using. Again, this is a leading symptom of the disease. It doesn't mean you're a bad person. It is how addiction takes over your mind.

What Is Your "Self-Talk"?

This exercise will help build your self-awareness about your addiction. Answer the following questions as best you can. Be honest with yourself.

➤ What signs are there in your life that you might have the disease of addiction?

_____

_____

_____

➤ What kind of excuses have you made to yourself in order to keep using?

_____

_____

_____

■

Because addiction hasn't killed you yet, you still have a chance to escape. It is possible to recover, however hard and long the road ahead of you may be. Millions of people who were every bit as addicted as you are have quit and recovered. It takes courage and work. As you recover, the denial and delusion will begin to lift. Only then will you realize how very sick you were.

The experience of addiction is not yours alone. It has three common, identifiable characteristics.

1. Addiction involves an unusual relationship with an activity or chemical—*an obsession*. When you're not doing it, you're thinking about it. It's the only thing that matters. You will pull away from family, friends, and everything else that was once important to you as the addiction consumes you. Getting and using is all you think about.

2. You *lose control,* but not all the time. This makes you think you're "managing" the addiction. Committing crimes to get money to buy illegal substances—and thereby risking incarceration—is out-of-control behavior. Being unable to stop, when you know you're in a tornado that's destroying everything of value in your life, is out-of-control behavior.

3. Even if you're able to stop for a time, you always *relapse.* Relapse—using again after stopping for a while—is bound to happen without proper support and treatment. Studies of addicts have proven that you can't quit on your own. It simply doesn't happen. You need help from others to break the cycle of addiction.

What is this addiction cycle?

- You experience pain, usually chronic (which means it happens on a regular basis) emotional pain. →

- You feel no good, worthless, and you can't stand that. →

- Your chronic inner pain feeds your need for feeling good, even if only for a short time. →

You need help from others to break the cycle of addiction.

- So you use. You take a drink, use another drug, or take part in addictive activities (sex, gambling, raging, etc.). →

- But instead of easing your pain, this behavior makes you soon feel worse. In your body, hangovers and other withdrawal symptoms happen. Emotionally, you feel shame for what you've done and who you are. Mentally, you see your life falling apart—relationships failing, jobs being lost, debts mounting, and so on. →

- All of these things make you desperate to use. And you start all over again.

Figure 3
CYCLE OF ADDICTION

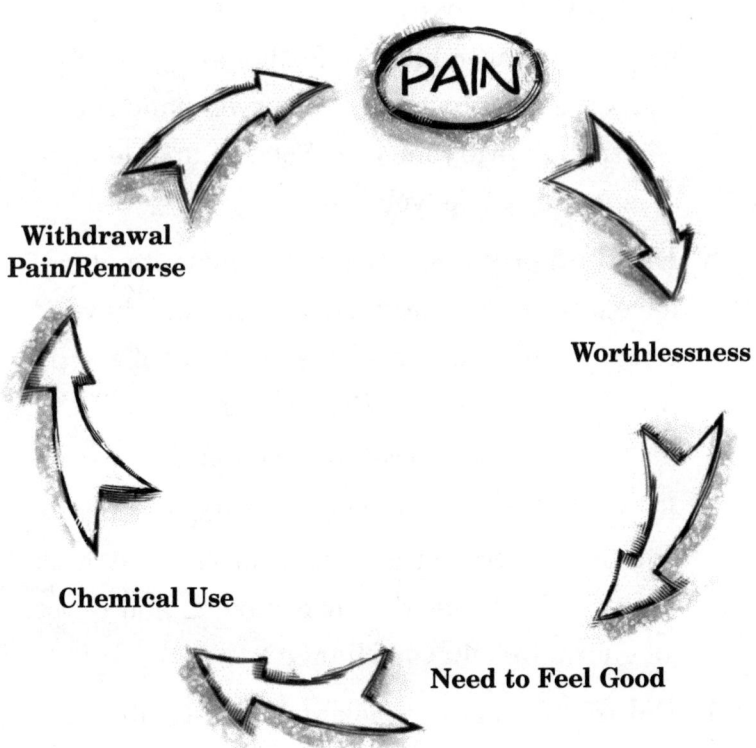

The Nine Symptoms of Addiction

Every illness has symptoms, and addiction is no exception. The nine general symptoms of addiction are

1. **Alcohol- or drug-oriented lifestyle.** The addictive substance becomes the center of your life. It is what you care about most. You choose friends who share your addiction and avoid people who don't. You go places where drugs or alcohol are available.

2. **Mental obsession.** All your thoughts are focused around using.

3. **Emotional compulsion.** You get uncomfortable and frustrated when you can't use. You need to use more and more to feel better.

4. **Low image or overinflated image of yourself.** You swing between thinking you're no good and worthless to feeling arrogant. You think that you have all the answers and are better than everyone else. You are unable to accept yourself as you are.

5. **Rigid negative attitudes.** Because you don't have compassion for yourself, you don't have compassion for other people. So, you believe the world is a bad place. When criminal activity results, you see no reason to change.

6. **Rigid defenses.** You deny your dependence on and the consequences of your alcohol and other drug use. You defend your behaviors and resist all efforts to help you change.

7. **Delusion.** You can't look at the truth about yourself. So, you ignore how your addiction has damaged your life. You say everything is fine. You blame any problems in your life on others.

8. **Powerlessness.** The addiction takes you over completely. You can't stop, and you can't ask for help, either. Even if you change for a short time, you relapse.

9. **Physical symptoms.** Your body tolerates larger and larger amounts of alcohol or other drugs. You need to use more and more to prevent withdrawal symptoms. You begin to forget everything but the high. You experience an all-consuming craving.

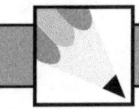 **EXERCISE 35 EXERCISE**

Your Addiction Symptoms

Answer the questions below as honestly as possible.

➤ Which of the nine symptoms of addiction have you experienced in the past?

_____

_____

_____

➤ What symptoms are you experiencing now?

_____

_____

_____

You can't look at the truth about yourself. So, you ignore how your addiction has damaged your life.

In short, addiction is an illness with clear symptoms. These include preoccupation with use, blackouts, increased drug tolerance, and physical conditions such as the shakes. The disease of addiction is chronic (meaning it's with you constantly). It creates permanent changes in your brain. As a result, it's progressive. That means it gets worse and worse unless you're treated. You lose all your good relationships and end up behind bars. And then you die. Untreated, addiction will kill you.

You don't have to go that route. You *can* recover. To start, you need to understand the disease—what it does to your brain and body.

What Alcohol and Other Drugs Do to Your Brain and Body

What alcohol and other drugs do to your body is complicated. They create permanent physical and chemical changes. Because of this, you can never again carry on "normal" use of your chemical of choice or of *any* addictive substance. Staying away completely is the only cure. It may sound impossible to you right now, but it's the only way to a better life.

Think of it this way. If you put a cucumber in a jar of vinegar, leave it there just a little while, and then take it out, it's still a cucumber. It hasn't turned into a pickle yet. But if you put a cucumber into that jar and leave it there long enough, at some point, it will become a pickle. It's hard to say when that happens, but after it does, you know it's not a cucumber anymore. More important, once it's pickled, it can never go back to being a cucumber.

Addictive substances make permanent changes in your brain chemistry. That is why recovery requires total abstinence. And these brain changes make you addicted to any chemical, not only the one you first became addicted to.

Most of your good feelings come from an area of the brain known as the "pleasure pathway." When something good happens, your brain makes chemicals that make you feel happy. This is the area of the brain that alcohol and other drugs affect, giving you an extra burst of pleasurable feelings.

But these feelings do not last. By the time the drug leaves your body, your brain has stopped producing its pleasure chemicals. That's when you go into withdrawal. A downward spiral begins. The more drugs you take, the fewer pleasure chemicals your brain produces on its own. This means you need more and more drugs to feel the pleasure. You swing from extreme highs to extreme lows. Your brain can't keep its balance. You're addicted, and there's no going back to "normal" use. You are physically, chemically unable to drink alcohol or use other drugs without having your brain immediately respond in an addictive way. This has nothing to do with willpower. It's basic brain chemistry.

It's also body chemistry. Addiction damages your body, too. Alcohol poisons all of your body's organs and systems, especially your liver, stomach and intestines, lungs, heart and blood vessels, and brain. It lowers your sex drive, causes birth defects, and increases your risk of heart attacks. Other drugs poison your body just as much, damaging your heart, kidneys, liver, and brain.

Why Do Addicts Relapse?

One of the main causes of relapse is not understanding the permanent physical changes addiction causes in your brain and body. After you haven't used for a while, you feel healthy. You feel good. You think you're cured and can handle the substance safely. You can't. Your brain switches instantly into an addictive mode. With just one use, you're addicted again.

To recover, your brain needs time to find its right balance in creating its own pleasure chemicals. While your brain and body are healing, you won't feel right. You'll go through the pain that drove your addiction. This is withdrawal. It's part of the process your brain needs to go through to relearn how and when to create its own pleasure chemicals. It must experience the pain to get back into the healthy habit of not depending on dangerous addictive substances for pleasure.

The best treatment for withdrawal is to not use any addictive substances and to take care of your body. You need lots of exercise, sleep, food, and water to help your brain and body heal.

Body and Brain Addiction Symptoms

This exercise is designed to help you learn more about your symptoms of addiction.

➤ What are your physical symptoms?

_____   _____

_____   _____

_____   _____

➤ What are your emotional symptoms?

_____   _____

_____   _____

_____   _____

➤ What are your mental symptoms?

_____   _____

_____   _____

_____   _____

➤ What negative things are happening in your life?

_____

_____

_____

The most obvious symptom of addiction in your life right now is that you're here behind bars. Addiction and crime have come together in your life. You need to understand how this happened and what you must do to change your situation and your future.

How Drugs and Crime Go Together

Drugs and crime go hand in hand. You know this. Addicts commit crimes to get alcohol or other drugs—to get and to pay for them. They also commit crimes while using alcohol or other drugs. Some of the most horrible crimes are committed during blackouts. *Blackout* does not mean passed out or unconscious. It means that after the high, the person has no memory of what he or she said or did during the blackout period.

For the criminal-addict, the excitement of committing crimes again is one of the major causes of using chemicals again. For the addict-criminal, using chemicals again will lead back to criminal activity.

These closely connected behaviors grow from closely connected thinking patterns. Addicts use their thinking patterns to justify and maintain addiction. Criminals use basically the same thinking patterns to justify and continue committing crimes—violating other people and their property. But the thinking patterns of addicts and criminals are pretty much the same.

These thinking patterns set the stage for addiction and crime. Both behaviors can seem like "spur of the moment" actions, but this is not true. The addict's and criminal's entire way of thinking makes addiction and criminal acts unavoidable. Addictive and criminal thinking patterns are like laying the wood for a bonfire and then pouring gas all over it. The slightest spark—a resentment, a grudge, a craving, feeling attacked—can start a huge blaze.

Why are the thinking patterns of addicts and criminals so similar? One reason is that both try to take shortcuts to excitement and pleasure. The problem is, sooner or later it always backfires. Shortcuts aren't successful for very long.

As both an addict and a criminal, you attempt to get your emotional needs met through chemicals, force, or crime—something outside of you. You look outside yourself for satisfaction, for ways to make yourself feel good. Even when that seems to work, it never lasts very long. That's because the only way to find long-term satisfaction is to look inside, at your thinking and your attitude. By doing this, your satisfaction with life will last as long as you want.

Because your mental map gives rise to both your addiction and your criminal behavior, your recovery depends on developing an alternative mind map to guide you. You need to shift your thinking patterns. Then, you will no longer set up bonfires for yourself, leaving you vulnerable to the slightest spark.

This means changing your thinking.

Recovery isn't about how not to use drugs. It's about learning how to live comfortably without having to turn to them.

Thinking Report

1. **Event** _____
   _____

2. **Thoughts** _____
   _____

3. **Feelings** _____
   _____

4. **Behavior** _____
   _____

5. **Can you identify a core belief?** _____
   _____

6. **Alternative thoughts** _____
   _____

7. **Alternative behavior** _____
   _____

Thinking distortions _____

Thinking patterns _____

Tactics _____

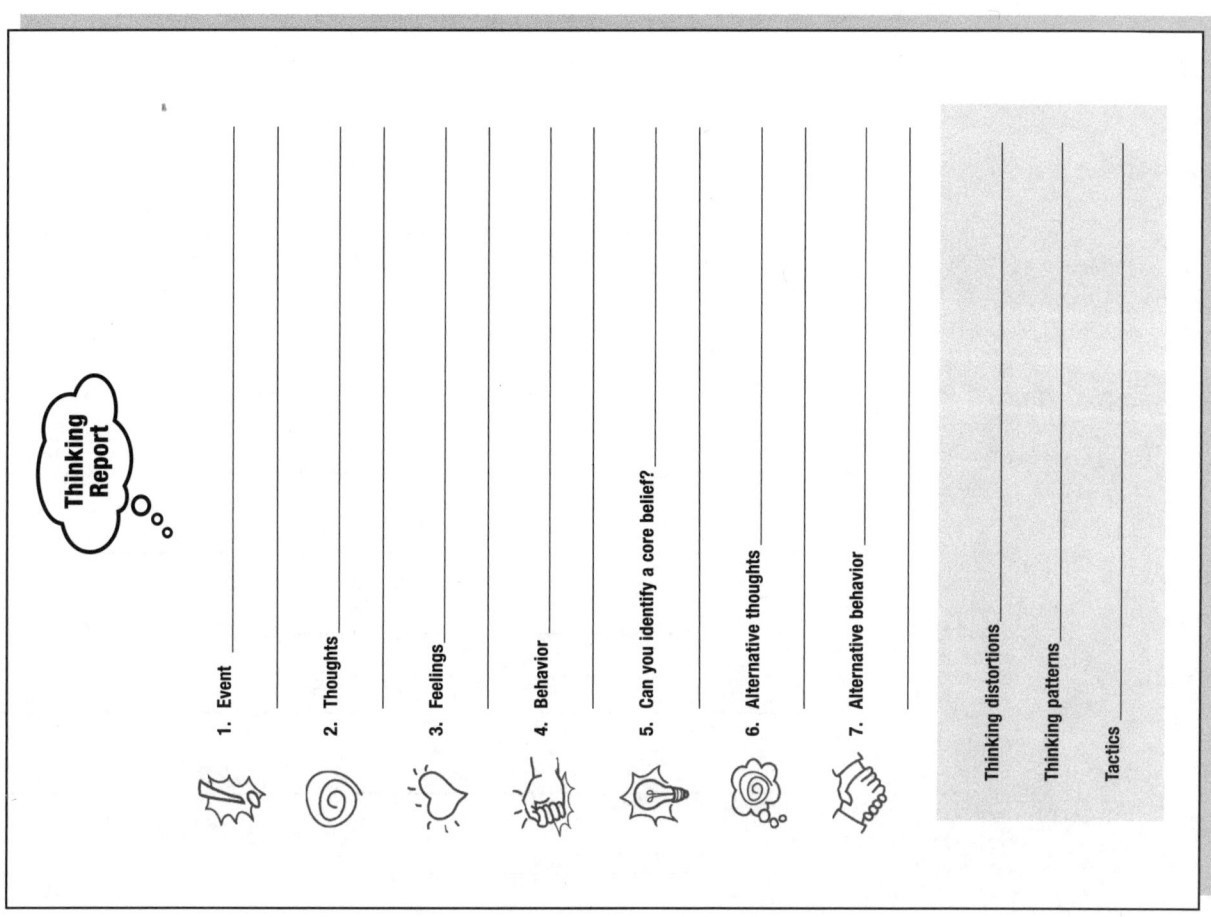

Thinking Report

1. Event _____

2. Thoughts _____

3. Feelings _____

4. Behavior _____

5. Can you identify a core belief? _____

6. Alternative thoughts _____

7. Alternative behavior _____

Thinking distortions _____

Thinking patterns _____

Tactics _____

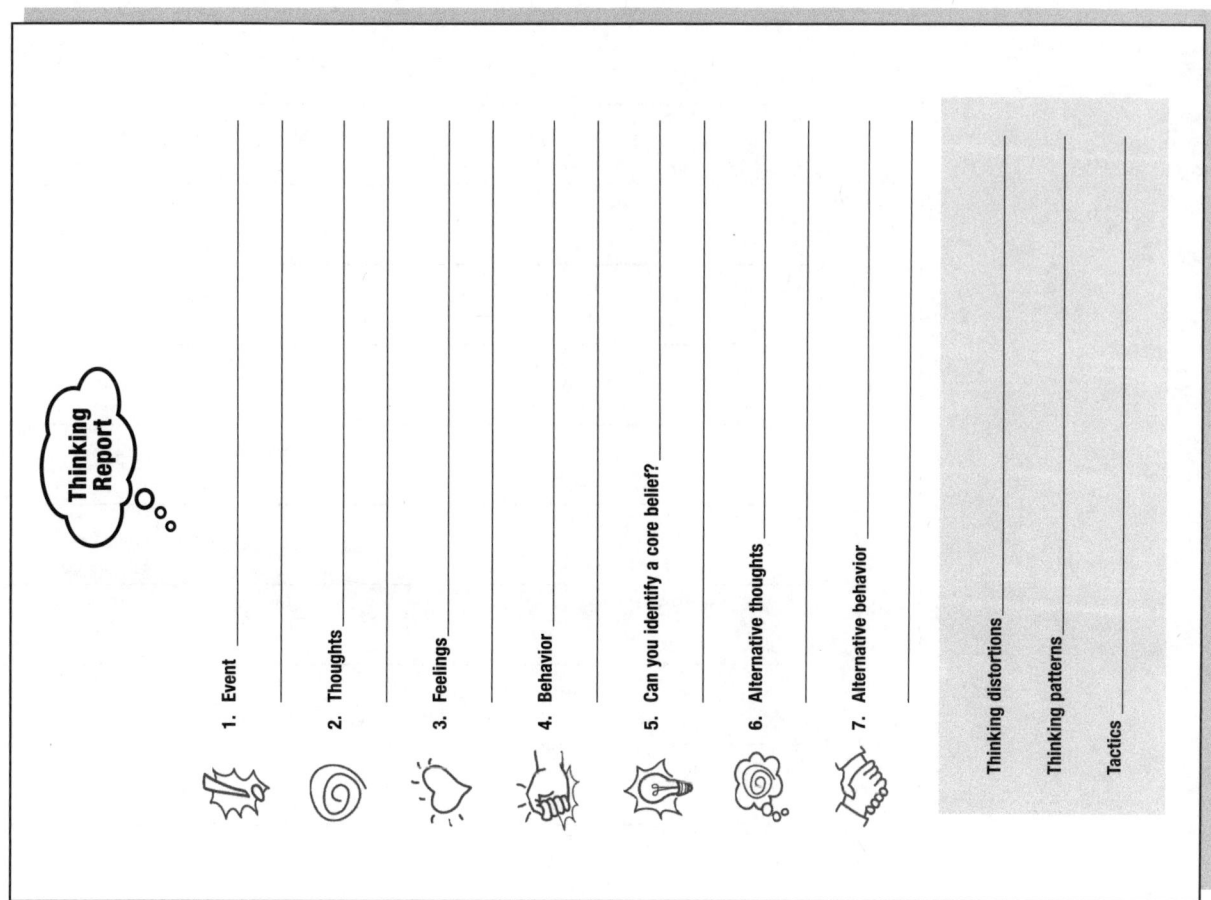

Thinking Report

1. Event _____

2. Thoughts _____

3. Feelings _____

4. Behavior _____

5. Can you identify a core belief? _____

6. Alternative thoughts _____

7. Alternative behavior _____

Thinking distortions _____

Thinking patterns _____

Tactics _____

NOTES

NOTES